Schiffer Military History
Atglen, PA

COLLECTORS GUIDE TO U.S. MILITARY WAR

DOGS OF WWII

[VOLUME·I]

ROBERT
ROSENKRANS

ACKNOWLEDGEMENTS

The Author would like to thank the following people for their assistance and contributions to this book: Hayes Otoupalik for the loan of many very scarce war dog items. Jim Whitehead of Bitterroot photography for his professional photographic skills. My wife Maria Rosenkrans for her assistance with this book.

DEDICATION

This book is dedicated to my best friend,
ROBERT ROSENKRANS SR.

PHOTOGRAPHS

Photographs are from contemporary and internet sources plus the authors collection. All pictures used are for identification purposes only and any infringement of internet copyright is unintentional.

Book Design by Justin Watkinson.

Library of Congress Control Number: 2011933826

Printed in China.
ISBN: 978-0-7643-3949-3

We are always looking for people to write books on new and related subjects.
If you have an idea for a book please contact us at the address below.

Published by Schiffer Publishing Ltd.
4880 Lower Valley Road
Atglen, PA 19310
Phone: (610) 593-1777
FAX: (610) 593-2002
E-mail: Info@schifferbooks.com.
Visit our web site at: www.schifferbooks.com
Please write for a free catalog.
This book may be purchased from the publisher.
Please include $5.00 postage.
Try your bookstore first.

In Europe, Schiffer books are distributed by:
Bushwood Books
6 Marksbury Avenue
Kew Gardens
Surrey TW9 4JF, England
Phone: 44 (0) 20 8392-8585
FAX: 44 (0) 20 8392-9876
E-mail: Info@bushwoodbooks.co.uk.
Visit our website at: www.bushwoodbooks.co.uk
Try your bookstore first.

CONTENTS

INTRODUCTION

War dogs have played an important role in the United States Military since WWI to the present day. WWII was the beginning for the K-9 corps as we know it today. War Dogs served in all theaters of operation during the war. There were 9295 sentry dogs trained for duty during the war; most went to the U.S. Coast Guard for shore duty. 571 dogs were trained as scout dogs. 268 were trained as sled and pack dogs. 151 were trained as messenger dogs and 140 were trained as mine dogs. The USMC effectively trained just over 450 dogs for combat at Camp Lejeune. The faithful service of the K-9 in WWII showed the War Department that a well trained dog had a multitude of uses in the military.

My great love for dogs and collecting interest led me to this book project. The goal is to share my collection, and at the same time to inspire others to keep the memory of war dogs alive by starting their own war dog collection.

PERIOD WAR DOG PHOTOS

CHAPTER 1

Lt. Arthur Murtha receives "Beauty" from Louis Brenner. This reception station was set up on the hotel Commodore roof in New York City, New York, by Dogs for Defense. Lt. Murtha and another soldier accompanied "Beauty" and several other dogs to the War Dog Reception and Training Center at Front Royal, Virginia. *Acme photo*. 29 April 1943.

A reluctant owner of a German Sheppard donates his K-9 to the Dogs For Defense program. *U.S. Army photo.*

Ten year old Paul Conners of Dorchester, Massachusetts, says goodbye to his pet Irish setter "Brownie" at a coast artillery post near Boston, Massachusetts. *AP wire photo.* 10 October 1942.

Five year old Carol Sims and her eight year old brother Paul Sims Jr. say goodbye to their German Shepherd "Silvers". Corporal R. J. Mason took Silvers with 36 other dogs to be shipped by rail from Chicago, Illinois, to Fort Robinson, Nebraska, where they were taught sentry duty for the U.S. Army.
AP wire photo. 2 October 1942.

Arizona prison officials donated "Wally", a blood hound, to the U.S. Army. Wally was trained at Fort Robinson for U.S. Army guard duty. Wally's trainer, Corp. William Winderlich, brought her from Fort Robinson, Nebraska, for the Colorado kennel show in Denver. *AP wire photo.* 25 September 1942.

This is a very interesting post card showing the various breeds that Dogs for Defense inducted into service. *Authors collection.*

The front gate of Fort Robinson Dog Reception Center.
Authors collection. 1944.

This is a photo of Officers and NCOs assigned to the war dog training and reception center at Fort Robinson, Nebraska late in WWII. Pictured from left to right: Don Stuber, Austan Manley, Billy Thomason, Lt. Laporta, Major Powers, Pat Notara, Pete Prindle, Jimmy Hughes, and Louis Koeler. *Authors collection.*

Off leash training at Fort Robinson.
Authors collection. 1944.

SSGT Leonard Fullerton and Arnold Swartz training a messenger dog at Fort Robinson. *Authors collection*. 1944.

SSGT Leonard Fullerton on the left training with an unknown soldier at Fort Robinson. The sign reads: MESSENGER DOGS DO NOT HANDLE OR SPEAK TO DOGS. *Authors collection*. 1944.

Sgt. Werner instructs dog handlers on the proper care of War Dogs while stationed at Fort Robinson, Nebraska. *International News photo*. March 1945.

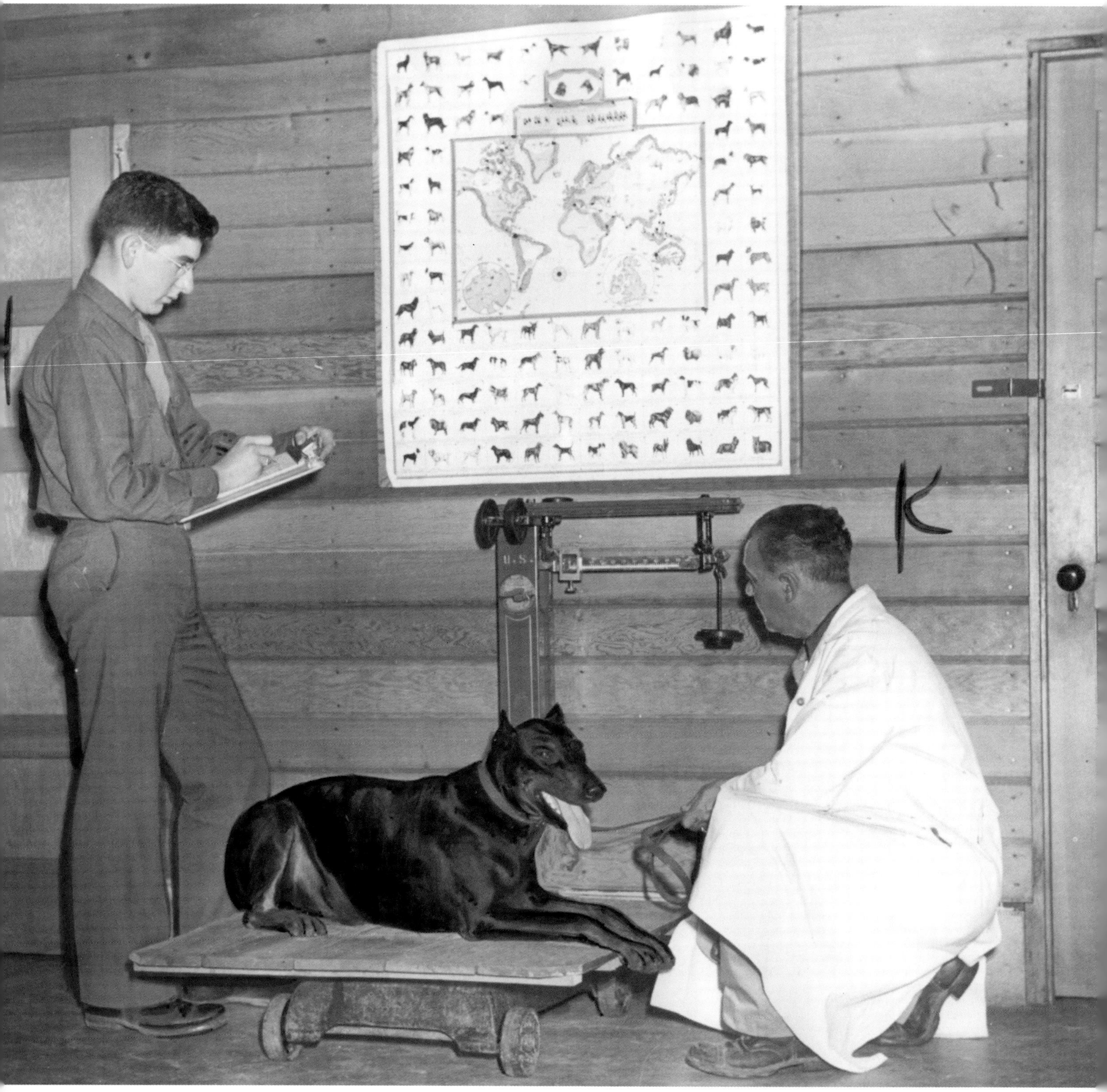

Even the war dog's weight went into the records. Through the animals' service, accurate records were kept so that the dogs could be returned to their rightful owners after the war. U.S. Army Signal Corps photo. March 1944.

This was part of the War Dog Sentry Unit at Mitchel Field, Long Island, New York. The handlers and K-9s are ready for inspection before going on their sunset to sunrise tour of duty. *Associated Press photo*. December 1942.

Weekly aggression keeps dogs in peak condition. US Army photo.

These sled dogs were being trained for duty in the Antarctic for rescue of downed airmen. *U.S. Army Air Forces photo.*

PFC Richard Large and Cpl. Robert Robinson were on duty at an advanced American base in the Aleutians. *Associated Press photo*. April 1943.

U.S. Army veterinarian bandages a wound on a sentry dog. *U.S. Army Signal Corps photo.*

Rin Tin Tin III showed how a trained Army dog would find a wounded soldier and would stay with him until stretcher bearers could remove him from the battle field. *Associated Press photo*. December 1942.

Army dogs and their handlers boarded a ship in the Los Angeles Port of Embarkation to sail for duty overseas. *U.S. Army Signal Corps photo*. January 1945.

American Infantrymen and their K-9s were ferried across one of the numerous river crossings as the MARS Task Force pushed into Burma. *U.S. Army Signal Corps photo*. December 1944.

This pack dog is attempting to carry a 1919A4 .30 caliber machine gun. The photo was taken along a lake at the base of the White Mountains, New Hampshire. *U.S. Army Signal Corps photo*. 1942.

SSGT Stanley Nevak, in the lead, was assigned to the Chineek Kennels in Wenalancet, New Hampshire, for testing of pack dogs. The photo was taken along a lake at the base of the White Mountains, New Hampshire.
U.S. Army Signal Corps photo. 1942.

U.S. Army Medical Corps unit on a training exercise near Wonalancet, New Hampshire used Siberian Huskies to pull dog sleds with doctors, nurses and medical supplies.
Associated Press Photo. February 1943.

CPL Peter Edman feeds his K-9 "Duke" chow in a U.S. Army helmet. The chow was a specially prepared dehydrated horse meat mixture. The photo was taken at Myitkyina, Burma. *U.S. Army Signal Corps photo.* September 1944.

CPL Carlos Valenzuela and his K-9 "King" at the point on patrol in New Guinea. *Associated Press photo*. September 1944.

CPL Charles Williams, of an infantry unit somewhere in Burma, fits his War Dog with custom made shoes. Dog shoes were designed after it was found that long hikes over jungle terrain cut dogs' feet badly enough to put them out of service. *U.S. Army Signal Corps photo*. 1944.

"Skipper", an Army K-9, received treatment for a gun shot wound in the lower jaw at a field hospital on Luzon. His wounded master, T/5 Frank Oliver, assists the medical corpsman with his good arm. Skipper was wounded in action at Balete Pass, near Baguio on Luzon, when he warned 25th Division infantrymen of an approaching Japanese patrol in the hills. *Acme News Pictures Inc*. April 1945.

Military Policeman PFC Robert Young and his K-9 "Trix" are guarding a military installation somewhere in France. *AP Wire photo*. August 1944

A War Dog "Kane" and CPL Jess Cowan go on patrol somewhere in the China-Burma-India theater. After CPL Cowan volunteered for the K-9 corps he enlisted his own dog Kane. Then they served together in the CBI. *U.S. Army Signal Corps photo*. July 1944.

96th Infantry Division dog handlers are headed for the front lines on Okinawa. *International News photo*. May 1945.

Sgt Lew Reeve of Austin, Minnesota, was the head trainer for the Panama Canal Zone. He was demonstrating the obedience of the dogs by walking over them after their handlers have commanded them to remain in position. *International News photo*. January 1943.

Dogs and handlers in a parade somewhere in Panama. They were used to guard military installations of the Panama Canal Zone. *Associated Press photo*. January 1943.

War Dogs waiting their turn at the obstacle course. *Authors collection*. July 1943.

Private John Kavanaugh and a K-9 "Rex" on guard duty somewhere in the Panama Canal Zone. *International News photo*. January 1943.

This is a mystery photo. The dog handler was dressed in a U.S. Army uniform while performing shore duty. This duty was for the U.S. Coast Guard only. Why was a U.S. Army PFC on shore duty with a B.A.R.? This is the only known photo with a WWII dog handler carrying a B.A.R. *Authors collection.*

Sgt J.W. Mehren and his German Shepherd dog were the guests of honor at a Rotary luncheon in Chicago after returning from sentry duty with the U.S. Army in New Caledonia. *APW Wirephoto*. 1944.

The U.S. Army experimenting with parachutes for War Dogs at Andrews Field, England. *AP Wirephoto*. September 1943.

"Topper", a K-9, proudly displayed his Honorable Discharge after serving with the U.S. Army as a sentry dog. *Authors collection*. February 1945.

War Dog show, Newport News, Virginia. *U.S. Army Signal Corps photo*. 23 February 1945.

War Dog show, Newport News, Virginia. *U.S. Army Signal Corps photo.* 23 February 1945.

War Dog show, Newport News, Virginia. *U.S. Army Signal Corps photo*. 23 February 1945.

Company B, M.P.s in drill formation at a War Dog show held at Casino Park, Newport News, Virginia. *U.S. Army Signal Corps photo*. 10 March 1945.

President Roosevelt met with Captain Jackson Boyd, who was the commanding officer of the War Dog Training Company at Camp Lejeune, N.C. *USMC photo*. December 1944.

“Bismarck” was one of the sentry dogs that helped U.S. Marines guard the Naval ammunition depot at Mare Island. Captain T.J. Palmer was the officer in charge of dog training at Mare Island. *USMC photo*.

Doberman-Pinschers on recruiting duty with Platoon Sergeant Edward Krajewski at Central Division Headquarters in Chicago. Doberman-Pinschers that qualified for service needed to meet the following requirements: male, stand 27 inches high from floor to top of shoulder, and weigh 70 pounds or over. All dogs that were accepted by the Marine Corps were trained at the Devil Dog School, Camp Lejeune, North Carolina. *USMC photo*. March 1944

USMC War Dogs entering their kennels at Camp Lejeune, North Carolina. *USMC photo*. May 1944.

K-9 recruits at Front Royal, Virginia, learning the command "sit". *International News photo*. September 1942.

“Andy” was part of the dog platoon at Bougainville and worked as a scout dog. Andy is pictures with one of his handlers, PFC Robert Lansley. *USMC photo*. February 1944.

"Jack", a USMC Marine K-9, was shot in the back by a Japanese sniper while carrying a message. Even though Jack was wounded, he still delivered his message. He is pictured with one of his handlers, PFC Finley. *USMC photo.* July 1945.

"Caesar", a Marine Corp K-9, was taken back to the rear for medical treatment after being wounded at the front lines on Bougainville. *USMC photo*. March 1944.

"King", a K-9, wasn't mentioned in casualty lists from Iwo Jima. But if any dog deserves honorable mention, it was King. This heroic War Dog suffered eight shrapnel wounds in the heavy fighting on Iwo Jima. Bandaged at a first aid station, King continued to do his duty. He was shown with his handler, Marine Pvt. Steven Hruby. *International News photo*. March 1945.

"Peppy," a USMC war dog, was listed as missing in action for three days during front line action on Guam. "Peppy" found his way back to his unit after being shot in his left ear. "Peppy"'s handler, PFC Goldblatt, is wearing an empty 1919A4 machine cartridge belt as a waist belt. Marines were very good at improvising. *USMC photo.*

USMC devil dogs on duty at Bougainville. *USMC photo.* February 1944.

USMC devil dogs on duty at Bougainville. *USMC photo*. February 1944.

USMC Corporal and his K-9 are on guard duty at an unknown USMC supply outpost. *USMC photo*. November1943

During the Bougainville Campaign "Liney", a Marine Corp K-9, picked up the scent of two Japanese snipers on the front lines. Liney is shown with one of his handlers, Pfc. Robert Forsyth. *USMC photo*. February 1944.

"Lady", a USMC K-9, barks goodbye to more than 300 of her former shipmates on the battleship *New York* docked at San Pedro, California. Lady was returning home for discharge after more than 25,000 miles at sea. Lady had two stars on her Pacific theater ribbon for the Iwo Jima and Okinawa campaigns. She had been promoted to First Sergeant by her commanding officer. She is shown with her owner, USMC first sergeant Cappel. *U.S. Navy photo*. September 1945.

Sgt Robertson takes care of "Tiny", a K-9 who was born on Guadalcanal to USMC War Dog "Ruff", also in the photograph. *Associated Press photo*. May 1944.

A Marine handler, PFC Broadus H. Blakely, tells his K-9 "Prince" that the Japanese have surrendered. *USMC photo*. August 1945.

Veterans of the Bougainville fighting were honored by a review of the K-9s that were training at Camp Lejeune, North Carolina. *International News photo*. June 1944.

These Marine dogs' duties were mainly to scout ahead in daytime and to perform outpost guard duty at night somewhere in the South Pacific. The dogs also performed a valuable service by guarding the handlers while they slept. *International News photo*. August 1944.

A dog handler is giving first aid to his dog after a training accident. *National Archives photo.*

Captain Raymond Mauerman was a chief training officer of the Coast Guard Dog Patrol. He examined a pair of new canvas boots which were designed to protect the War Dogs' feet from cuts with oyster shells while on long beach patrols. *U.S. Coast Guard photo.*

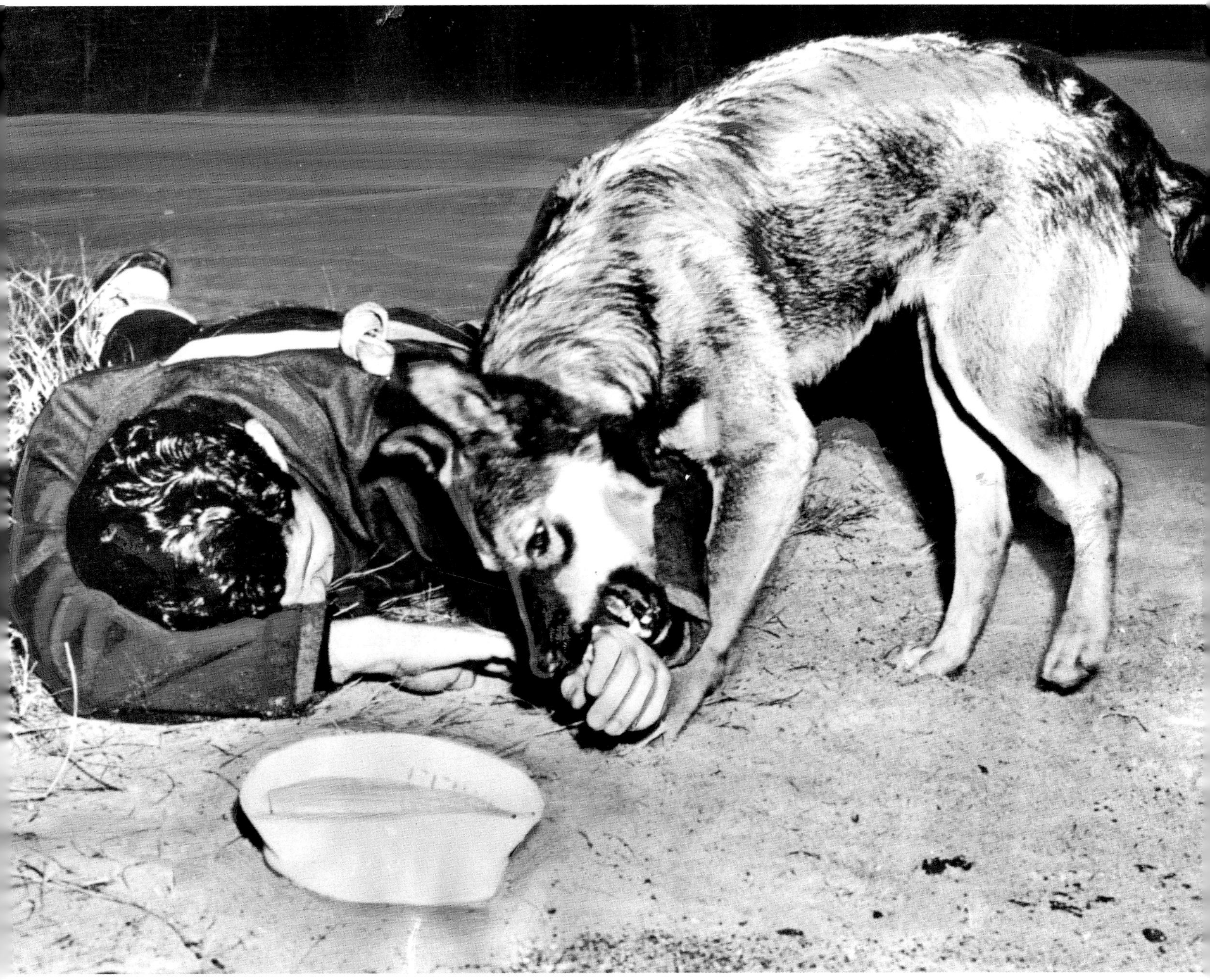

"Nora", a K-9, saved the life of Coast Guardsman Evans Mitchell on an isolated North Carolina beach. Mitchell fainted while on night patrol. Nora found him and tried in vain to raise him. She then took Mitchell's cap to a Coast Guard station to summon help. *U.S. Coast Guard photo*. March 1944.

U.S. Coast Guardsmen and their dogs become proficient at the obstacle course. *U.S. Coast Guard photo*. February 1943.

"Skipper" was a Coast Guard sentry dog who was demonstrating his leaping ability at the Golden Gate Park dog demonstration. *San Francisco Examiner*. April 1944.

Graduation day for U.S. Coast Guard War Dogs and handlers. Most USCG War Dogs were used for stateside shore duty, with only a small number being assigned to guard Naval installations in the South Pacific. *USCG photo.*

Graduates of the War Dog Training and Receiving Detachment at the U.S. Coast Guard Training Station, Curtis Bay, Maryland. *Authors collection*. 1944.

War Dog inspection in front of the kennels at the U.S. Coast Guard Training Station, Curtis Bay, Maryland. *Authors collection*. 1944.

Attack exercise during a USCG war dog demonstration at the USCG Air Station at Elizabeth City, North Carolina. *USCG photo*. September 4, 1944

Exterior view of the kennels at the U.S. Coast Guard Training Station, Curtis Bay, Maryland. *Authors collection*. 1944.

Interior view of the kennels at the U.S. Coast Guard Training Station, Curtis Bay, Maryland. *Authors collection*. 1944.

Aggression training at the U.S. Coast Guard Training Station, Curtis Bay, Maryland. *Authors collection*. 1944.

Graduation parade at the U.S. Coast Guard training station, Curtis Bay, MD. Note most dog handlers are carrying the Reising sub machine gun. *Authors collection*.

On a lonely Atlantic outpost, a Coast Guardsman and his alert K-9 partner were on the alert for suspicious activity. *U.S. Coast Guard photo*.

Lone sentry and K-9 somewhere on the West coast. Note: the only weapon the dog handler has is a .38 Victory model. *USCG photo*. 1944.

U.S. Coast Guard dog handlers during a training mission somewhere on the East coast. *USCG photo*. 1944.

U.S. Coast Guard Dog Patrol with a U.S. Navy patrol blimp in the background. *USCG photo*. 1944.

A great photo of a U.S. Coast Guard Beach Patrol. The handler was assigned a Reising submachine gun. *USCG photo*. 1944.

A U.S. Coast Guard trainee and K-9 doing some photo ops. *USCG photo*. 1944.

U.S. Coast Guard dog patrols practicing boat landing maneuvers. *USCG photo*.

U.S. Coast Guard Dog Patrol on training maneuvers. Note: the lead dog handler is using a U.S. Cavalry WWI era 45 Auto cavalry holster. The U.S. Coast Guard was not a front line fighting unit, so they routinely received outdated equipment. *USCG photo.*

U.S. Coast Guard dog handlers work on basic aggression training. The dog and handler look to be almost the same size. This practice was stopped after the war and a larger dog would be paired with a larger handler. *USCG photos*.

Coast Guardsman Michael Planchak and his K-9 "Jack" were en route to perform sentry and scout duty somewhere in the Pacific. *U.S. Coast Guard photo*. 1944.

U.S. Coast Guard dog handlers work on advanced aggression training with a firearm. *USCG photo*.

This K-9 member of the Coast Guard Dog Patrol was on duty against spies and saboteurs. *U.S. Cost Guard photo*.

"Mitsie", a K-9 war hero, was a mascot for New York VFW post #500. Mitsie served in the Coast Guard for 18 months and was the first dog to be discharged from Coast Guard service. Mitsie's owner, John M. Behan, on the left, wrote the book *Dogs of War* in 1946. *Acme News photo*. March 1945.

"Juneau" was a Coast Guard Husky that pulled sleds loaded with supplies for Coast Guard outposts in the Arctic during WWII. *USCG photo*.

WAR DOG EQUIPMENT

CHAPTER 2

WATERPROOF DOG BLANKET

came in three sizes: small, medium and large. The outside of the blanket was made with a standard OD poplin and the inner part was made of standard wool blanket material. This model was used by the U.S. Army and the U.S. Coast Guard. *Authors collection*.

USMC WATERPROOF DOG BLANKET

came in three sizes: small, medium and large. The outside of the blanket was made with a standard OD poplin and the inner part was made of standard wool blanket material. This model was used by the U.S. Army and the U.S. Coast Guard. *Authors collection*.

THEATER MADE USMC DOG BLANKET was made from a USMC overcoat and a set of shelter half straps. *Authors collection.*

THEATER MADE 82nd AIRBORNE PARADE BLANKET. A small detachment of War Dogs were trained to jump with airborne troops. The war ended before they could be used, but the unit still participated in several parades at the end of the war. *Authors collection.*

STANDARD U.S. CAVALRY HORSE BRUSH

was issued to dog handlers during WWII. Since large quantities were stored at Letterkenny Army Depot in Carlisle, Pennsylvania, at the beginning of WWII, the War Department decided to save money and resources by reissuing the horse brushes as a dog brush. *Authors collection*.

U.S. CAVALRY FEED PAN AND WATER BUCKET

were reissued to the K-9 corps to save money and metal during the war.
These were used at stateside training camps and were not intended for combat use. *Authors collection*.

U.S. ARMY DOG SHIPPING CRATE

was used to ship dogs to and from training facilities. Dogs were also shipped in these crates via ship to Europe and the Pacific. Only one dog was shipped in each crate. The dimensions are: Height 31" by Width 24" by Length 40". The USMC dog's shipping crate was the same size but of slightly different construction than the Army's. *Authors collection.*

U.S. ARMY DOG CRATE

rear and side view. *Authors collection.*

CASUALTY DOG WOOD BRINSELL was a short stick that hung below the casualty dog's collar. When the dog found a wounded soldier on the battlefield, it would place the stick in his mouth and would then return to his master. This would let the handler know that his K-9 had found a wounded soldier.
Courtesy Hayes Otoupalik.

CASUALTY DOG SPECIAL TRAINING HARNESS was made from cotton webbing and was only used during training. *Authors collection*.

CASUALTY DOG LEATHER BRINSELL was the 2nd version which was adopted by the U.S. Army. This version was easier to carry by the soldier and was more durable in combat. *Courtesy Hayes Otoupalik*.

MESSAGE COLLAR

was used by messenger dogs. The collar comes with a rubberized piece of OD material that the message would be rolled up into to protect it from moisture. *Authors collection*.

WAR DOG PIGEON VEST

was designed so that a messenger dog could carry two pigeons to a remote area to support a tactical unit operating away from its own base. The training for this program took place at the Cat Island War Dog Training facility in Mississippi. These vests did not see combat service during WWII. *Courtesy Hayes Otoupalik*.

WAR DOG WIRE LAYING HARNESS was tested at the Cat Island War Dog Training facility using messenger dogs. Since a dog was a hard target to hit while running, the War Department experimented with this means of laying field phone wire in a combat zone. The wire was secured to a D ring at the top of the collar and the dog was then sent from one handler to another to lay the wire. *Courtesy Hayes Otoupalik.*

WAR DOG SPARE AMMUNITION PACK was experimental and probably did not see much if any combat service at all during WWII. The pack was made by using the inner parts from two M1928 haversacks. The pack could carry two bandoleers of rifle ammunition on each side. *Authors collection*.

WAR DOG PARACHUTE HARNESS was made by front line units of various components found in riggers' shops. The harness used a standard T5 reserve parachute. This was not an official design and the War Department did very little research into airborne deployment of War Dogs during WWII. *Authors collection*.

E12R8 DOG GAS MASK

was made from a coated canvas duck material. This mask used a single E32 series filter. Since the placement of the filter at the end of the mask made it easy for the dog to dislodge the mask, the E12R8 never made it out of the test phase. This is an extremely scarce mask because the Army only made a very small number of them for testing. *Authors collection.*

M6-12-8 DOG MASK

was the official War Dog gas mask adopted by the U.S. Army during WWII and stayed in service through the 1950s; it was declared obsolete in 1969. The M6 mask used two M12 filters. During trials of the M6 mask, mud and dirt would often clog the inlet holes. A mud guard (E4R2) was designed to fit over both filters' inlet holes to protect against blockage. This is also a scarce mask since a total of only 1409 were produced. *Authors collection.*

E12 SERIES CANVAS GAS MASK BAG

was carried by the dog's handler. *Courtesy Hayes Otoupalik.*

M6-12-8 GAS MASK BAG

was designed by the Chemical Warfare Service, which realized that War Dogs might be used during a sea invasion and went with a waterproof carrier. This carrier was also carried by the dog handler. *Courtesy Hayes Otoupalik.*

CHAINETTE AND CHOKE CHAIN

were both made of welded steel rings. The chainette, also known as a throwing chain, was used for correcting the dog at a distance from the trainer. These were only used for training and were not taken into combat. This choke chain was the second model and came in two lengths: 22" and 24". This choke chain was slightly cheaper to make than the chain choke collar. *Courtesy Hayes Otoupalik.*

WOOD SHIPPING CRATE FOR CHAINETTES

held 250 chains. *Courtesy Hayes Otoupalik.*

ALL PURPOSE HARNESS

was suitable for teaming in pairs. This harness is missing the leather collar. *Authors collection.*

LOW DRAFT WEB SIWASH HARNESS

was the favored harness by the U.S. Army Sledge Dog Program because of its light weight and ease of use. *Authors collection.*

LEATHER TANDEM HARNESS

was only used with the single tandem hitch. *Authors collection.*

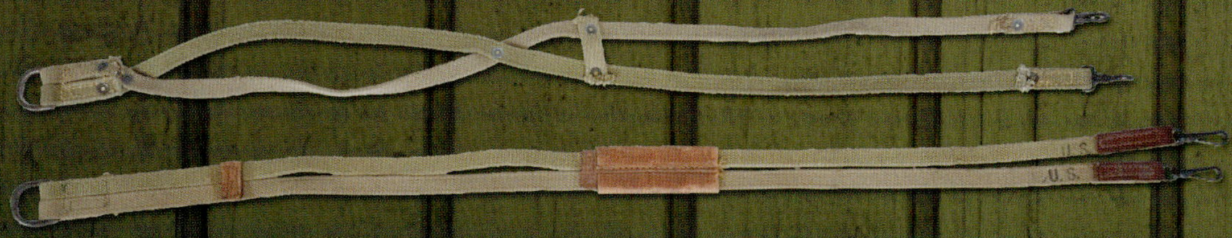

LIGHT DUTY SLED DOG HARNESSES

were used only when the dog was in camp, instead of actual sled harnesses, which were used for pulling the sled. The handler would attach the leash to the light duty harness to walk the dog around the camp. *Authors collection.*

STANDARD U.S. MILITARY MUZZLE

was issued to each dog handler, but most of the handlers threw them away after leaving training because it was too time consuming to put the muzzle on. It was easier to use the leather leash as an improvised muzzle. *Courtesy Hayes Otoupalik.*

STANDARD U.S. MILITARY LEASH, CHOKE CHAIN, AND BELT CARRIER

was issued to each dog handler for hanging it on the belt when the handler was not using his K-9. The leash was made of leather and measured 6' long. *Authors collection.*

NON-REGULATION U.S. MILITARY LEASH

was often manufactured at various military repair shops for dog handlers. This leash came with other period dog gear and was made of heavy canvas measuring 6' long. *Authors collection.*

CHAIN CHOKE COLLAR

was made of strong welded steel rings. Dog handlers complained that there were no visible markings on the dog to identify it as being a War Dog. The collar filled the need. *Courtesy Hayes Otoupalik.*

SPECIAL FLAT LEATHER COLLAR

for sentry, attack, and silent scout dog training. *Courtesy Hayes Otoupalik.*

25 FOOT LONG LEASH

was part of the basic training program equipment and was used for training the dog to stay and heal at a longer distance.
Courtesy Hayes Otoupalik.

12 FOOT STEEL TETHER CHAIN

was used to secure the dog to its house at War Dog Training centers.
Courtesy Hayes Otoupalik.

WAR DOG AGGRESSION TRAINING SUIT was very difficult to use due to its inflexibility, and trainers did not like to use these suits in the summer because they were really hot. This suit is missing the left arm and the head protector. *Courtesy Hayes Otoupalik*.

PORTABLE ARMY AND NAVY WEIGHT SCALES manufactured by Fairbanks were used by war dog reception centers during WWII to track the dogs' weight during training. The scale has a 300 pound capacity. The length is 27", the width is 15", and the height is 10". *Authors collection.*

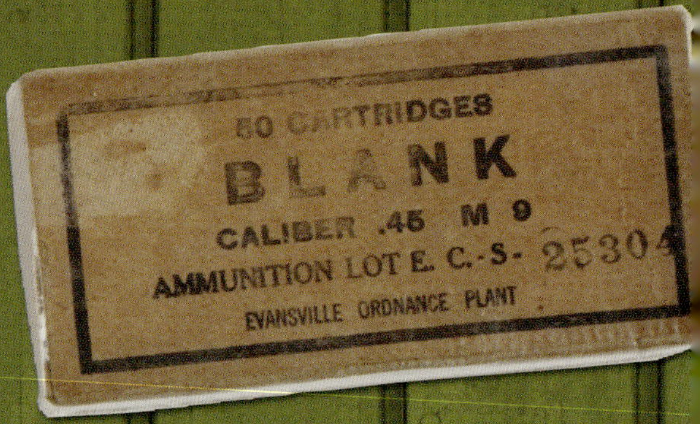

45 AUTO TRAINING BLANKS

were used in advanced aggression training to teach dogs not to fear the sound of gun fire. The blanks were made with a steel case to save brass and were manufactured at the Evansville Chrysler plant in Evansville, Indiana. *Authors collection.*

BOOKS AND MANUALS

CHAPTER 3

TENTATIVE HANDBOOK, WAR DOGS PARTS I & II were with **TENTATIVE TECHNICAL MANUAL WAR DOGS PART III** to produce **TM 396 WAR DOGS.**

Since the K-9 Corps was formed quickly, the two tentative manuals were used until TM 10-396 was finished. *Authors collection.*

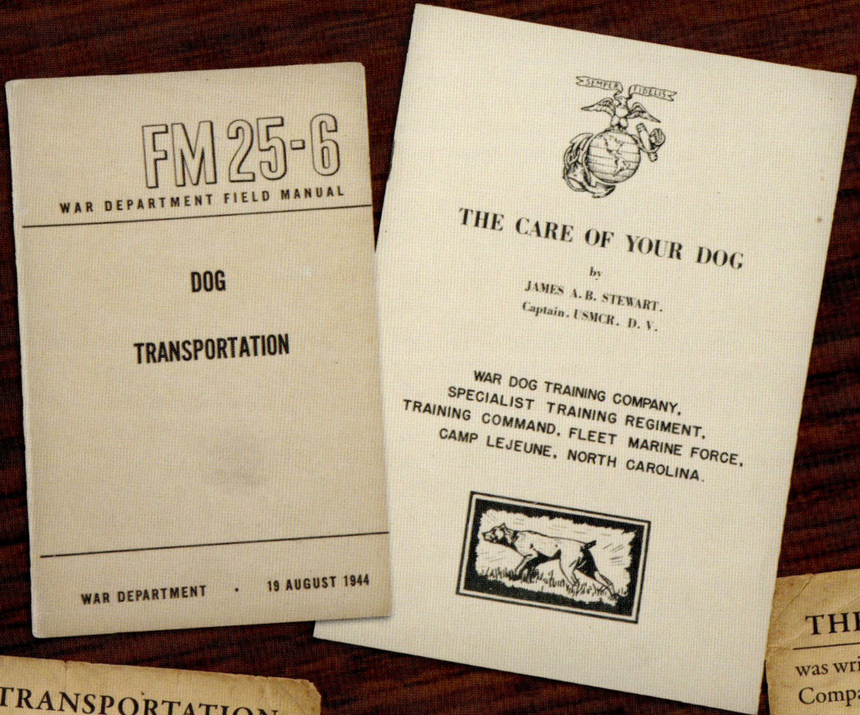

FM 25-6 DOG TRANSPORTATION contains information on training and deployment of sledge and pack dogs as a means of transporting people and supplies. *Authors collection.*

THE CARE OF YOUR DOG was written by the USMC War Dog Training Company at Camp Lejeune, North Carolina. The manual was written by Captain James Stewart D.V. This manual was only issued to USMC dog handlers and is scarce due to the very limited numbers that were printed. *Courtesy Hayes Otoupalik.*

FICTION BOOKS ABOUT WAR DOGS

that served in the U.S. Military during WWII. *Authors collection.*

CHILDREN'S NONFICTION BOOKS

depicting War Dogs of WWII. These books helped inspire many children to donate their dogs to Dogs for Defense for the War effort. *Authors collection.*

TROOPER
U. S. Army Dog
by
HELEN ORR WATSON
RED ROCK II
BRIG. GEN. WILLIAM R. WHITE
AND
FRANK CUNNINGHAM
VALIANT COMRADES
A STORY OF OUR DOGS OF WAR
RUTH ADAMS KNIGHT
Juggernaut of the Rangers
Paul Brown
Story by
Harold H.
Strickland
Pictures by Paul Brown
DOG OF WAR
FAIRFAX DOWNEY
Gulliver
JOINS THE ARMY

WAR TIME MAGAZINES

published articles about War Dogs because of their growing popularity in the military. *Authors collection.*

LUCKY THE OUTCAST MOVIE POSTER.

This patriotic movie is about a boy and girl that donate their dog to the war effort and the dog's service in the Pacific against the Japanese. The movie features Lionel Stander, Jerry Hunter, Sharyn Moffett, and Harry Davenport. The movie was produced in 1942 by Astor Pictures Corp. *Authors collection.*

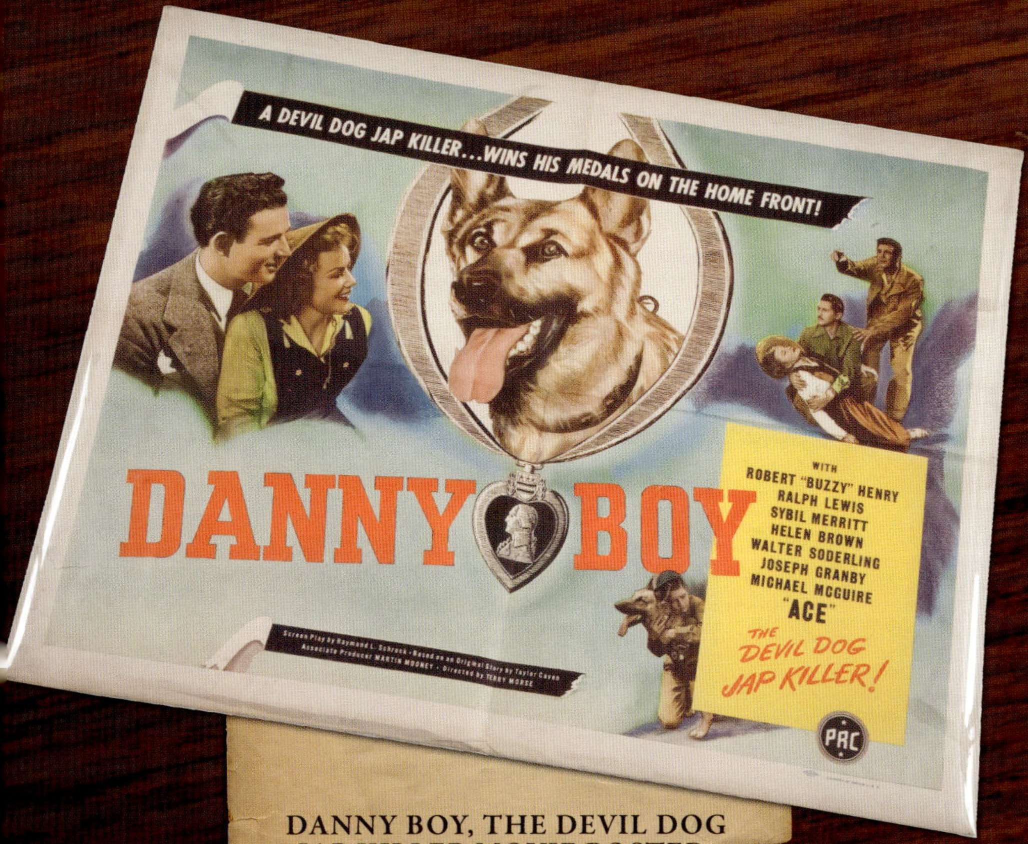

DANNY BOY, THE DEVIL DOG JAP KILLER MOVIE POSTER.

This war time movie depicts a dog's heroic life after his return from war dog service in the Pacific. *Authors collection*

MISCELLANEOUS WAR DOG RELATED ITEMS

CHAPTER 4

PERSONAL HYGIENE KITS

from various War Dog training centers.

SOURCE: *Authors collection.*

GUILD WAR DOG PICTURE PUZZLE

measures 16" by 20". It was produced by the Guild Company. The original picture that was used for the puzzle was painted by Hintermeister. His painting became very popular and was often used by Dogs for Defense as recruitment art work.

DOGS FOR DEFENSE GLASS ASH TRAY

was given for volunteer work with Dogs for Defense. DFD donated thousands of dogs to the War Department throughout the war.

SOURCE: *Authors collection.*

STERLING SILVER DOGS FOR DEFENSE PRESENTATION DISH

was one of the top awards that DFD gave to its members for service and recruitment. This dish was made by Black, Starr & Gorham and measures 2 ½" by ½".

SOURCE: *Authors collection.*

PAPER ITEMS

CHAPTER 5

DOGS FOR DEFENSE RECRUITING POSTERS measure 13 ½" by 22". These are two of four known recruiting DFD posters. *Authors collection.*

"Chubby" and his owner Margaret Cole pose with a Dogs For Defense recruiting poster, where "Chubby" was the model for the poster.
Authors collection. February 1944

DOGS FOR DEFENSE RECRUITING ADVERTISEMENTS from various magazines printed during WWII. These advertisements were sponsored by dog food companies. *Authors collection.*

WAR DOGS..
Wanted by the Army, Navy, Coast Guard and Marines!
Now serving with all of the U. S. armed services . . . War Dogs have proved themselves a valuable weapon for our fighting men. Keen of sight, hearing and scent . . . the K-9 Corps has distinguished itself by good work on sentry, communications, sledge and scouting duty. Today the Army, Navy, Coast Guard and Marines are all asking for more of these 4-footed fighters!
Your Dog May Serve His Country
It's not too late to enlist your dog for vital war work. Check these requirements to see if he can qualify: Dogs may be purebred or crossbred of breeds specified by the Armed Services; must be at least 20 inches high at the shoulder and weigh at least 50 lbs.; must not be storm shy or noise shy; must be at least 1 year old and not more than 5. Enlisting dogs for War Work is the duty of Dogs for Defense, Inc., a volunteer civilian organization. For complete information on enlisting a dog, send the coupon below.
ENLIST YOUR DOGS AND YOUR DOLLARS
DOGS FOR DEFENSE
D F D
DOGS FOR DEFENSE, INC.
PURINA MILLS, 1210 Checkerboard Square, St. Louis 2, Mo.
Please send me ☐ the official Dogs for Defense questionnaire for dog volunteers, ☐ A Dogs for Defense War Fund pledge and complete information about dogs in war work.
Name
Address
City
State
No. of Dogs
Breed
PUBLISHED IN THE INTEREST OF
DOGS FOR DEFENSE, Inc.
by Purina Mills. Makers of
PURINA DOG CHOW
PURINA
DOG CHOW

DOGS FOR DEFENSE RECRUITING ADVERTISEMENTS

from various magazines printed during WWII. These advertisements were sponsored by dog food companies. *Authors collection.*

ROVER DOESN'T LIVE HERE ANYMORE...
A Service Star for Rover...
HE'S IN THE ARMY, NOW!
ALL-OUT WAR is a dog's war, too. Thousands of "Rovers" the country over have already volunteered and are now in training camps or on duty with the U. S. Armed Forces. And it's serious business, too . . . they're being trained for sentry duty, communications, rescue, pack and sled work and other special services. The United States is now busy building the largest, finest corps of trained dogs in the world . . . many thousands of dogs will be needed by the Army alone. That means dog volunteers are needed now!
YOUR DOG MAY SERVE HIS COUNTRY
Dogs for the armed forces will be selected from dogs volunteered by patriotic dog owners the country over.
The requirements are simple: Dogs may be purebred or crossbred, must not be less than 18 inches in height at the shoulder, not storm shy or noise shy, not less than 1 year or more than 5 years old. Your dog will be well-trained, well-fed, and well cared for while he's serving Uncle Sam.
Enlisting dogs for war work is the function of Dogs for Defense, Inc., a volunteer, civilian organization indorsed by the American Kennel Club and officially approved by the War Department. If you are interested in enlisting your dog, or in making a cash contribution, send the coupon below for a dog questionnaire and complete information.
ENLIST YOUR DOGS AND YOUR DOLLARS
DOGS FOR DEFENSE
D F D
DOGS FOR DEFENSE, INC.
PURINA MILLS, 1210 Checkerboard Square, St. Louis, Mo.
Please send me ☐ the official Dogs for Defense questionnaire for dog volunteers, ☐ A Dogs for Defense War Fund pledge and complete information about dogs in war work.
Name..........
Address..........
City..........
No. of Dogs..........Breed..........State..........
PUBLISHED IN THE INTEREST OF
DOGS FOR DEFENSE, Inc.
by Purina Mills. Makers of
PURINA DOG CHOW
PURINA
DOG CHOW

CAT ISLAND WAR DOG RECEPTION & TRAINING CENTER

was located approximately 12 miles South of Gulfport, Mississippi, in the Gulf of Mexico. *Authors collection.*

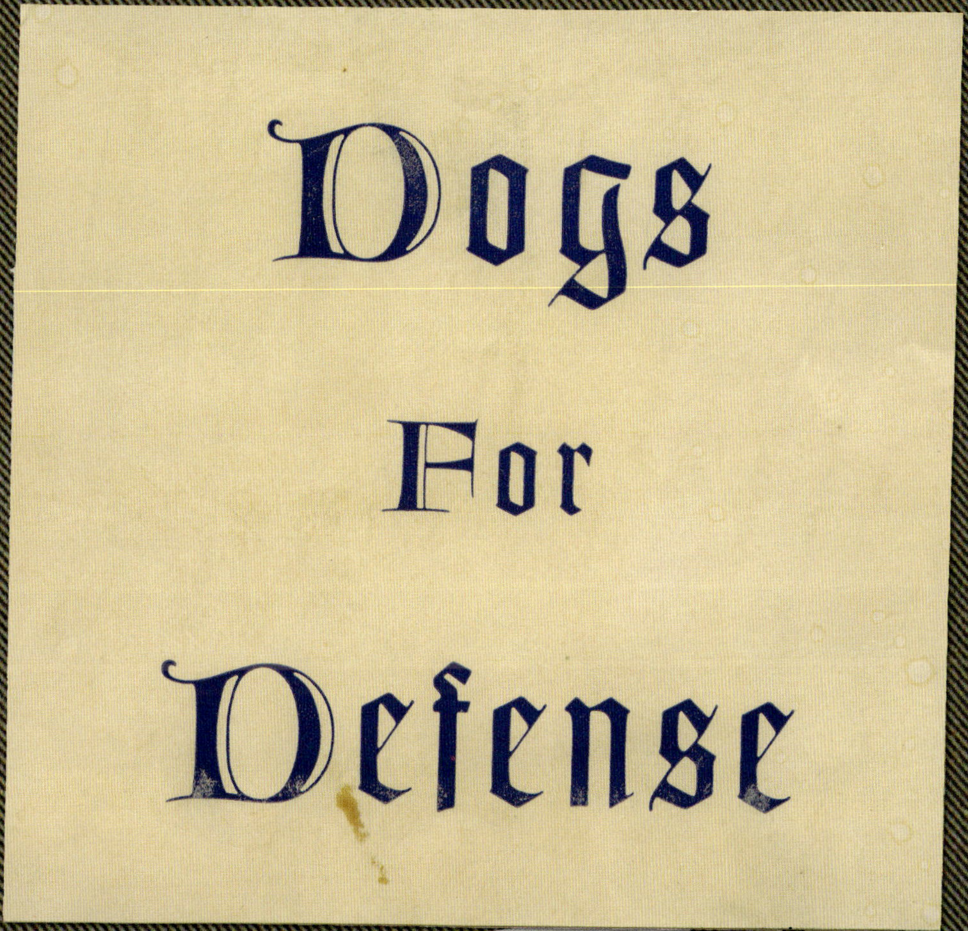
Dogs
For
Defense

DOGS FOR DEFENSE WINDOW STICKER was sent to the donor to be placed in the front window of their home to show that they donated a dog. *Courtesy Hayes Otoupalik.*

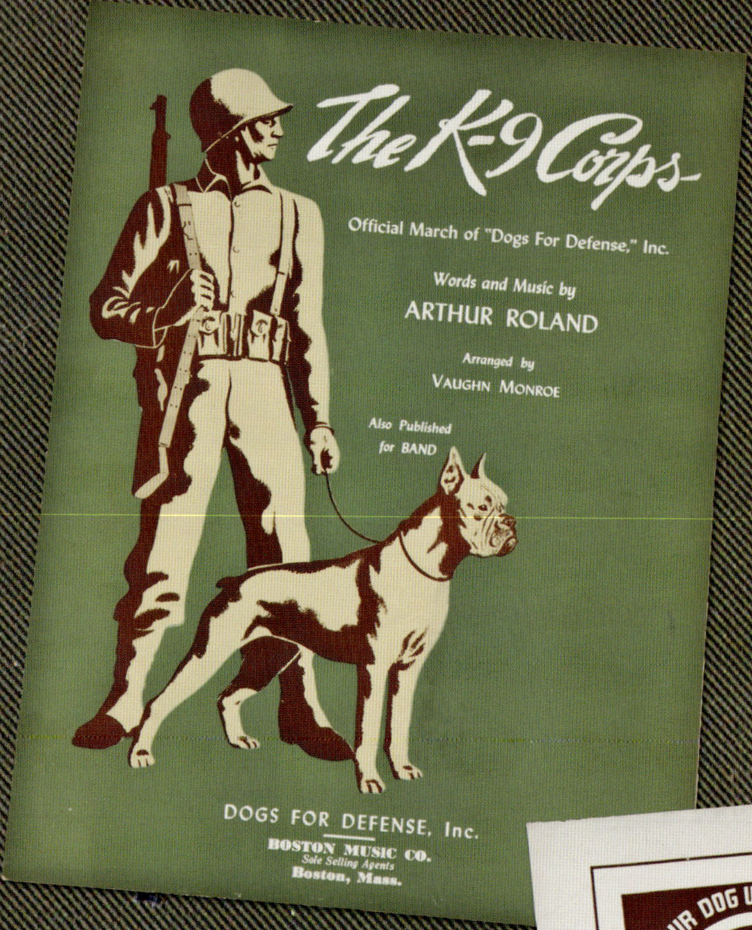

THE K-9 CORPS OFFICIAL MARCH OF "DOGS FOR DEFENSE". The back page contains a DFD recruiting poster. Words and music were written by Arthur Roland in 1943. *Authors collection.*

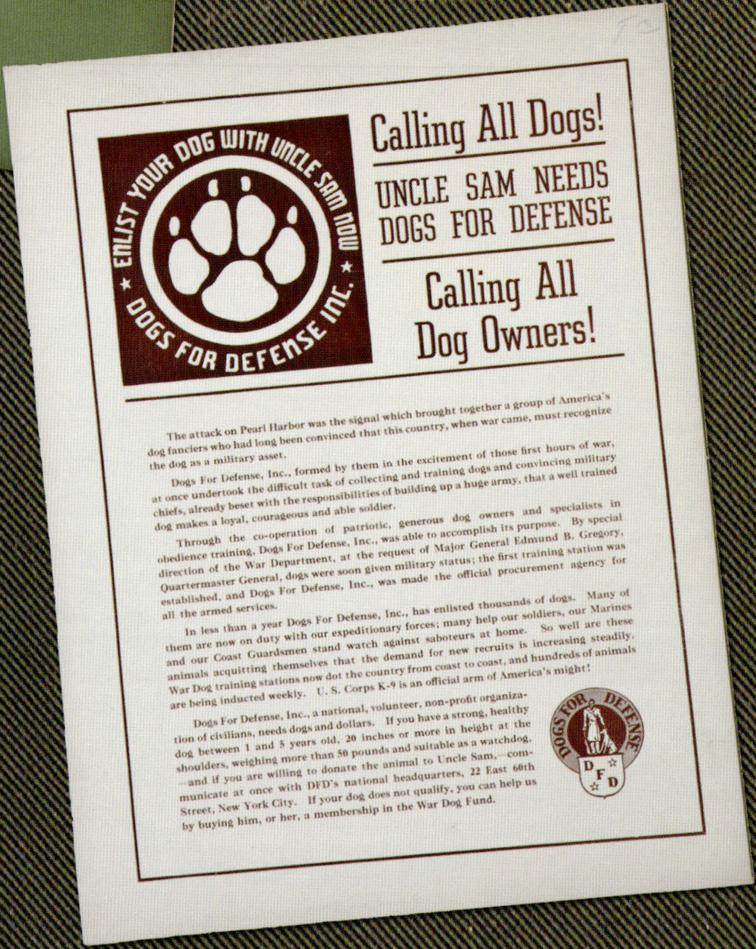

Calling All Dogs!

UNCLE SAM NEEDS DOGS FOR DEFENSE

Calling All Dog Owners!

The attack on Pearl Harbor was the signal which brought together a group of America's dog fanciers who had long been convinced that this country, when war came, must recognize the dog as a military asset.

Dogs For Defense, Inc., formed by them in the excitement of those first hours of war, at once undertook the difficult task of collecting and training dogs and convincing military chiefs, already beset with the responsibilities of building up a huge army, that a well trained dog makes a loyal, courageous and able soldier.

Through the co-operation of patriotic, generous dog owners and specialists in obedience training, Dogs For Defense, Inc., was able to accomplish its purpose. By special direction of the War Department, at the request of Major General Edmund B. Gregory, Quartermaster General, dogs were soon given military status; the first training station was established, and Dogs For Defense, Inc., was made the official procurement agency for all the armed services.

In less than a year Dogs For Defense, Inc., has enlisted thousands of dogs. Many of them are now on duty with our expeditionary forces; many help our soldiers, our Marines and our Coast Guardsmen stand watch against saboteurs at home. So well are these animals acquitting themselves that the demand for new recruits is increasing steadily. War Dog training stations now dot the country from coast to coast, and hundreds of animals are being inducted weekly. U. S. Corps K-9 is an official arm of America's might!

Dogs For Defense, Inc., a national, volunteer, non-profit organization of civilians, needs dogs and dollars. If you have a strong, healthy dog between 1 and 5 years old, 20 inches or more in height at the shoulders, weighing more than 50 pounds and suitable as a watchdog,—and if you are willing to donate the animal to Uncle Sam,—communicate at once with DFD's national headquarters, 22 East 60th Street, New York City. If your dog does not qualify, you can help us by buying him, or her, a membership in the War Dog Fund.

DOGS FOR DEFENSE
D F D

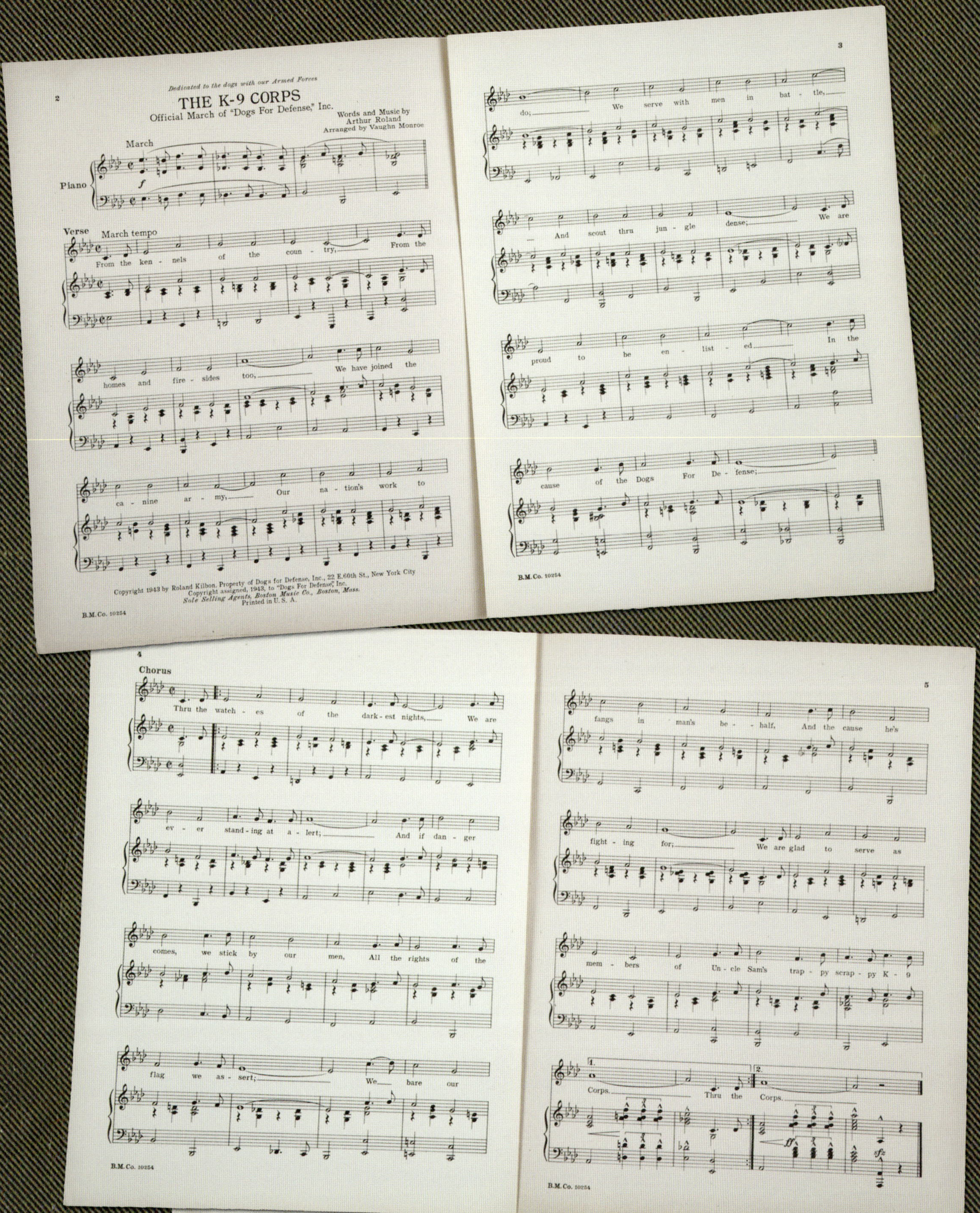

K-9 CORPS COMPLETE WORDS AND MUSIC.

Authors collection.

DOGS FOR DEFENSE ENLISTMENT APPLICATION

Authors collection.

ENLISTMENT APPLICATION

22 EAST 60TH STREET
NEW YORK CITY
PLAZA 9-6471

Breed

No. ....

Remarks
....

PLEASE DO NOT WRITE IN THIS SPACE

OWNER

Name ....

Address ....

....

....

Please Print Clearly

We greatly appreciate your offering us your dog to be trained for service with the United States armed forces, and ask that you fill out this questionnaire to help us determine its eligibility.

Breed .... Shoulder Height .... Age .... Call Name ....

Sex .... A. K. C. Reg. Name and Number (if available) ....

If bitch, has she been spayed? .... If not spayed, when was she last in season? ....

Has dog had permanent distemper inoculation? .... If so, when? ....

Has dog had distemper? .... If so, when? .... Has dog been examined recently and declared free of worms .... Has dog lived in kennel or house? ....

If house, how long? .... Is dog nervous? .... Does dog run away? ....

Is dog afraid of noise? .... Gun shy? .... Storm shy? ....

What is dog's attitude towards strangers? ....

Please furnish photograph or snapshot of dog. Have you a crate for shipping this dog? ....

General remarks (including health, disposition, training and special habits) ....

....

....

....

I am the owner of the dog described above, and hereby offer it unconditionally to DOGS FOR DEFENSE, INC. I understand that if this dog should be found unsuitable, it will be returned to me within a short time. I further understand that no commitment can be made as to the disposition of this dog after the war, but, if possible, I would like the following disposition to be made:

....

....

Date .... Signature ....

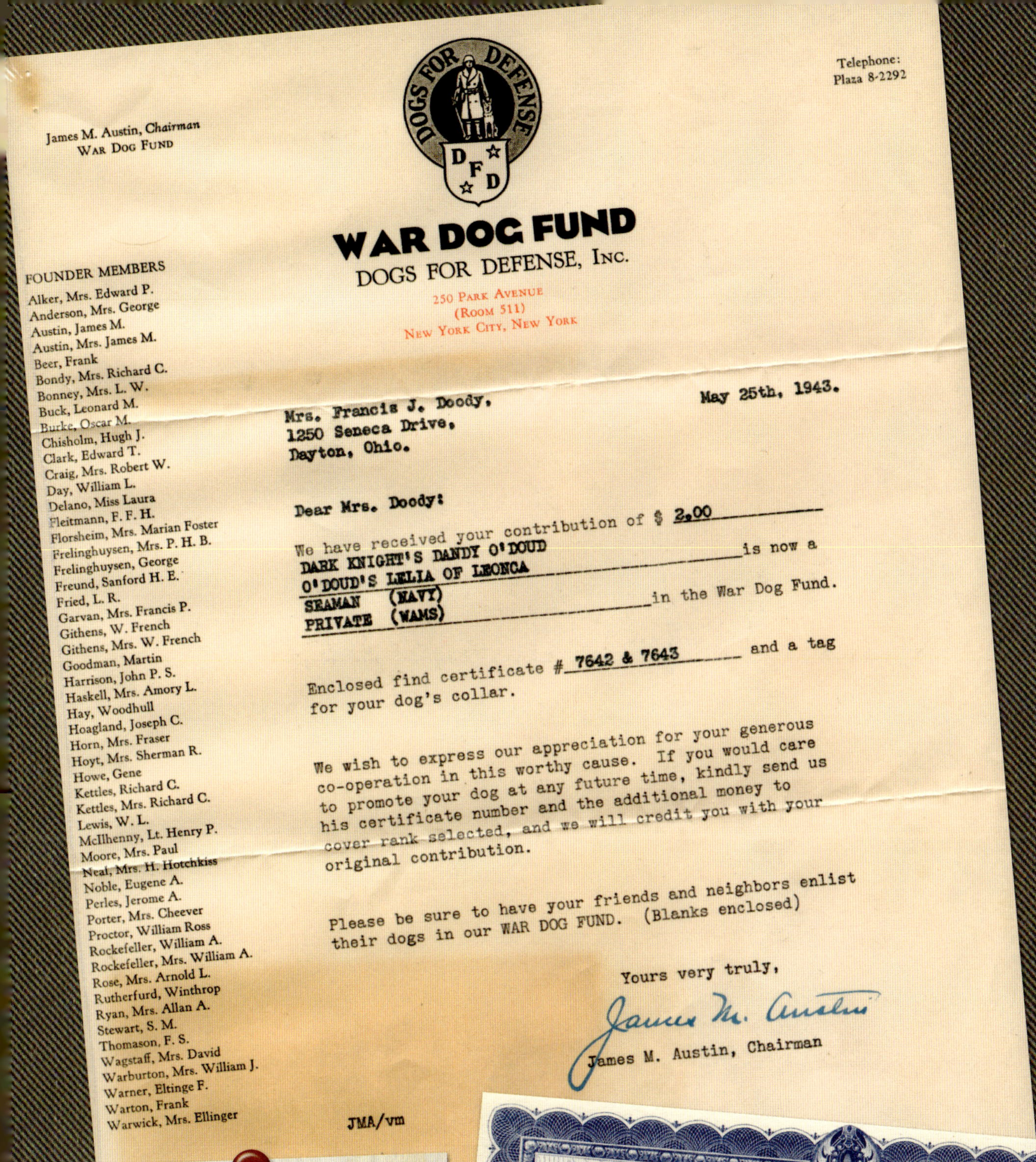

DOGS FOR DEFENSE

D F D

Telephone:
Plaza 8-2292

James M. Austin, Chairman
War Dog Fund

WAR DOG FUND

DOGS FOR DEFENSE, Inc.

250 Park Avenue
(Room 511)
New York City, New York

FOUNDER MEMBERS
Alker, Mrs. Edward P.
Anderson, Mrs. George
Austin, James M.
Austin, Mrs. James M.
Beer, Frank
Bondy, Mrs. Richard C.
Bonney, Mrs. L. W.
Buck, Leonard M.
Burke, Oscar M.
Chisholm, Hugh J.
Clark, Edward T.
Craig, Mrs. Robert W.
Day, William L.
Delano, Miss Laura
Fleitmann, F. F. H.
Florsheim, Mrs. Marian Foster
Frelinghuysen, Mrs. P. H. B.
Frelinghuysen, George
Freund, Sanford H. E.
Fried, L. R.
Garvan, Mrs. Francis P.
Githens, W. French
Githens, Mrs. W. French
Goodman, Martin
Harrison, John P. S.
Haskell, Mrs. Amory L.
Hay, Woodhull
Hoagland, Joseph C.
Horn, Mrs. Fraser
Hoyt, Mrs. Sherman R.
Howe, Gene
Kettles, Richard C.
Kettles, Mrs. Richard C.
Lewis, W. L.
McIlhenny, Lt. Henry P.
Moore, Mrs. Paul
Neal, Mrs. H. Hotchkiss
Noble, Eugene A.
Perles, Jerome A.
Porter, Mrs. Cheever
Proctor, William Ross
Rockefeller, William A.
Rockefeller, Mrs. William A.
Rose, Mrs. Arnold L.
Rutherfurd, Winthrop
Ryan, Mrs. Allan A.
Stewart, S. M.
Thomason, F. S.
Wagstaff, Mrs. David
Warburton, Mrs. William J.
Warner, Eltinge F.
Warton, Frank
Warwick, Mrs. Ellinger

Mrs. Francis J. Doody,
1250 Seneca Drive,
Dayton, Ohio.

May 25th, 1943.

Dear Mrs. Doody:

We have received your contribution of $ 2.00
DARK KNIGHT'S DANDY O'DOUD
O'DOUD'S LELIA OF LEONCA is now a
SEAMAN (NAVY)
PRIVATE (WAMS) in the War Dog Fund.

Enclosed find certificate # 7642 & 7643 and a tag for your dog's collar.

We wish to express our appreciation for your generous co-operation in this worthy cause. If you would care to promote your dog at any future time, kindly send us his certificate number and the additional money to cover rank selected, and we will credit you with your original contribution.

Please be sure to have your friends and neighbors enlist their dogs in our WAR DOG FUND. (Blanks enclosed)

Yours very truly,

James M. Austin

James M. Austin, Chairman

JMA/vm

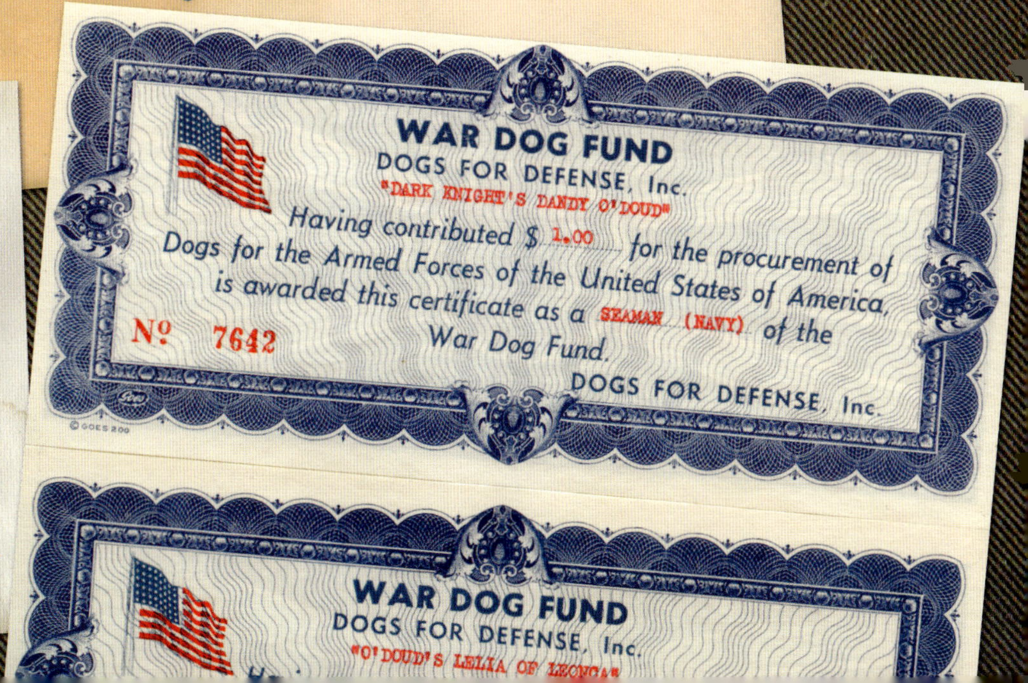

WAR DOG FUND
DOGS FOR DEFENSE, Inc.
"DARK KNIGHT'S DANDY O'DOUD"
Having contributed $ 1.00 for the procurement of Dogs for the Armed Forces of the United States of America, is awarded this certificate as a SEAMAN (NAVY) of the War Dog Fund.
Nº 7642
DOGS FOR DEFENSE, Inc.

WAR DOG FUND
DOGS FOR DEFENSE, Inc.
"O'DOUD'S LELIA OF LEONCA"

WAR DOG FUND CONTRIBUTION LETTER and WAR DOG FUND CERTIFICATE were given to financial donors by Dogs for Defense. Many dogs were rejected by DFD due to their small size or other reasons that made them incompatible with war service. Since the owners still wanted to participate, they would send a donation and receive a DFD package that contained the letter, certificate, and also a window sticker with a dog tag (shown in the next photo). By a specific sum of money donated, the donor could "pick the rank" of their dog. The more money they donated, the higher the rank. *Authors collection.*

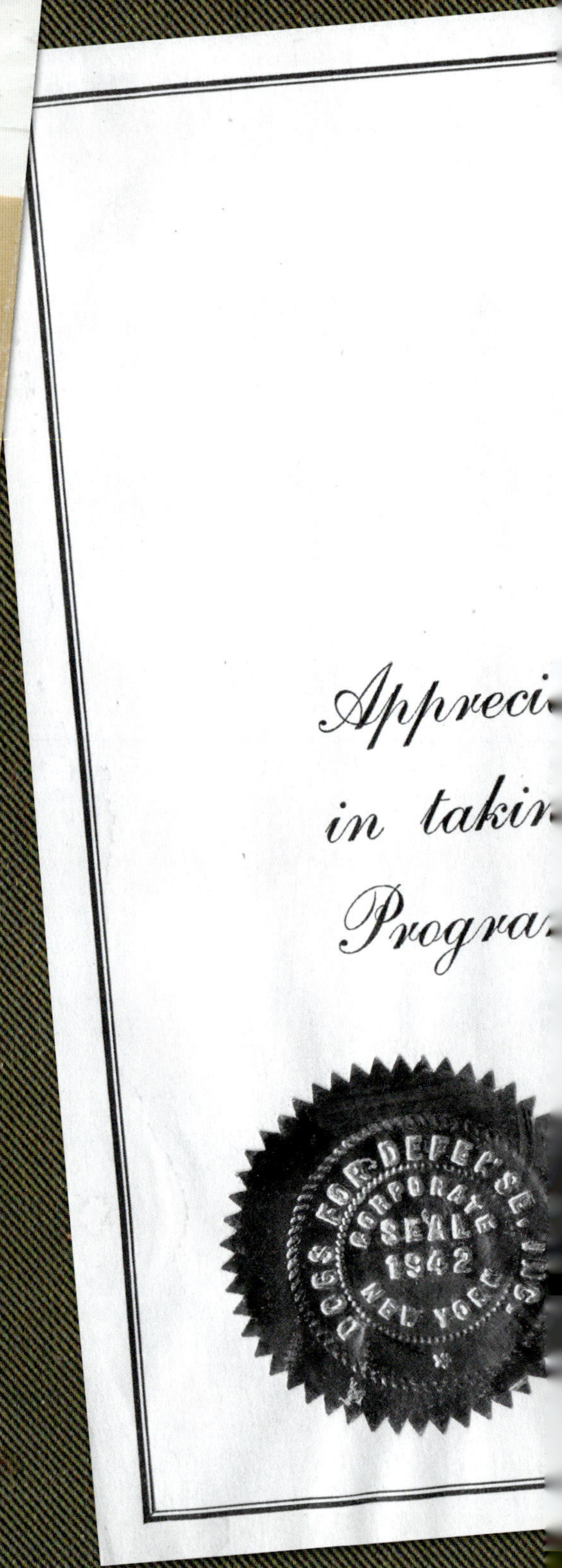

WAR DOG FUND WINDOW STICKER and DOG TAGS

were given to financial donors by Dogs for Defense along with the letter and certificate (see two previous photographs). The dog tags were made of cellulous and were worn by the donors' dogs. The sticker could be placed on the windshield of the donor's automobile or on the front window of the donor's house. *Authors collection.*

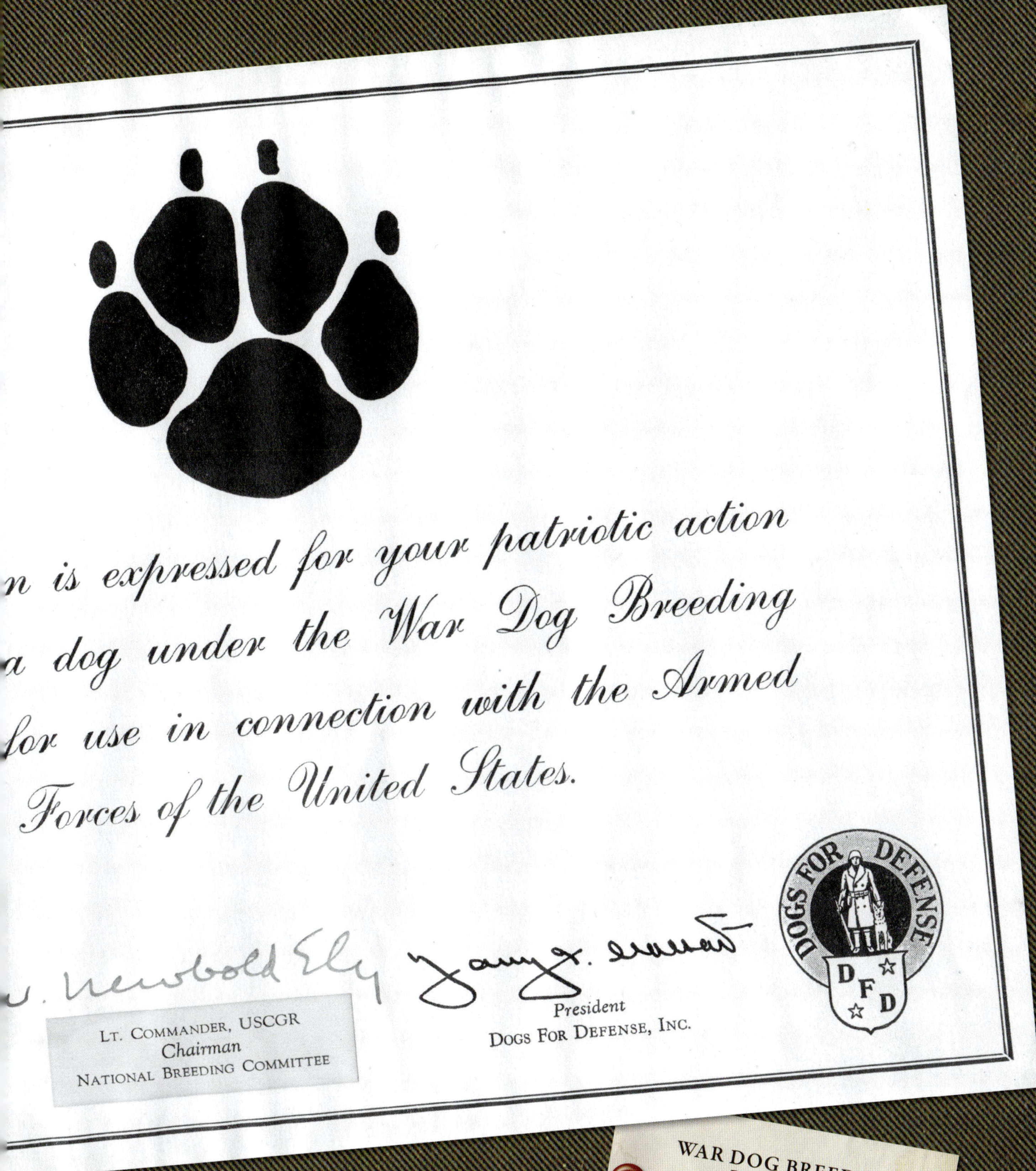

n is expressed for your patriotic action
a dog under the War Dog Breeding
for use in connection with the Armed
Forces of the United States.

Newbold Ely

Lt. Commander, USCGR
Chairman
National Breeding Committee

President
Dogs For Defense, Inc.

Dogs For Defense
D F D

WAR DOG BREEDING PROGRAM APPRECIATION LETTER was a certificate that was given by Dogs for Defense to breeders who participated in the program. *Authors collection.*

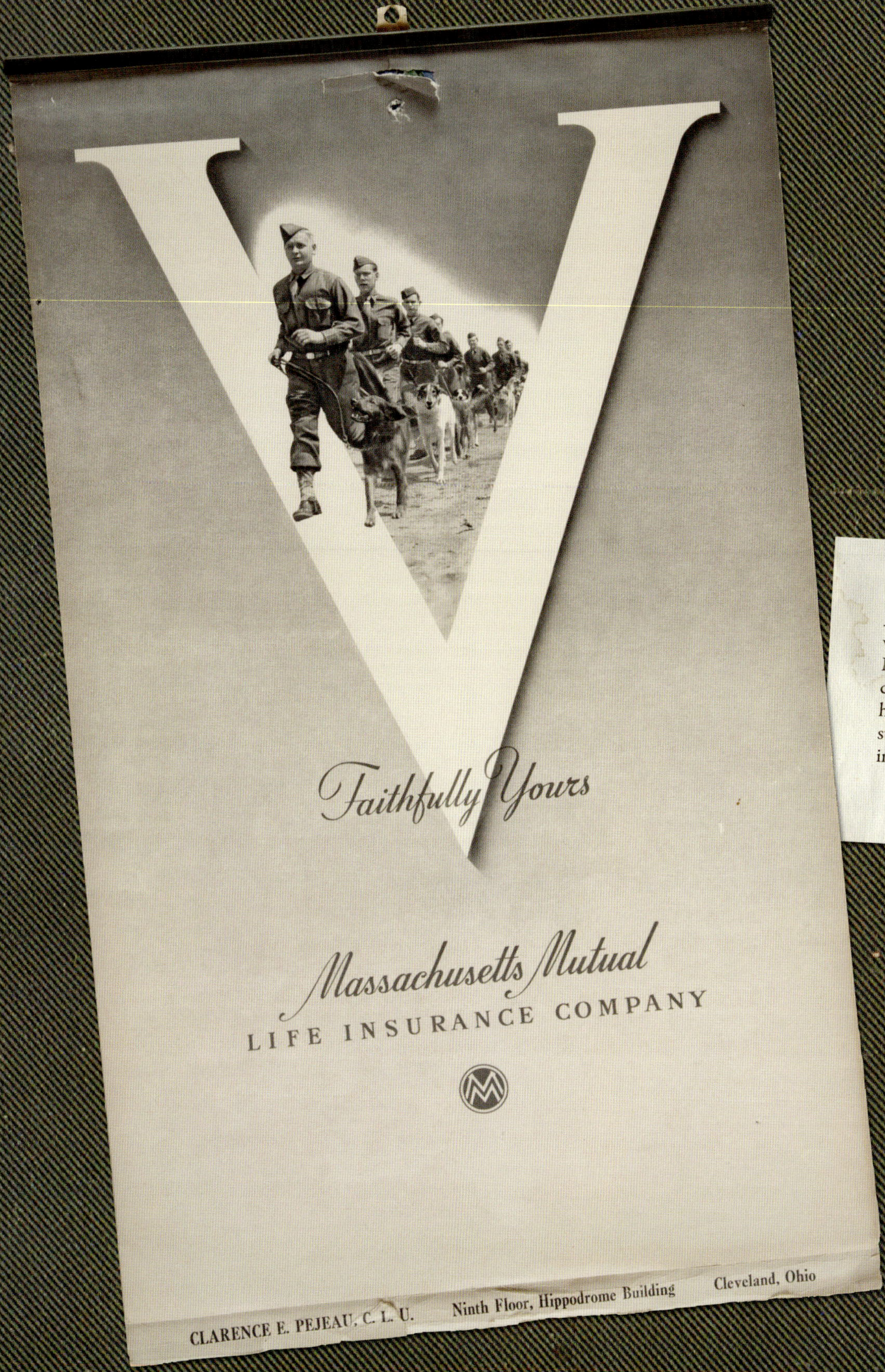

1944 VICTORY WAR DOG CALENDAR

was given out by the Massachusetts Mutual Life Insurance company to their customers. Many other company names have been found using this calendar to support the Dogs for Defense effort and inspire people to donate. The calendar measures 11 ½" by 20". *Authors collection.*

ENROLLMENT ACCEPTANCE U.S. COAST GUARD DOG PATROL CERTIFICATE was given to dog donors whose dogs were used by the U.S. Coast Guard. *Authors collection.*

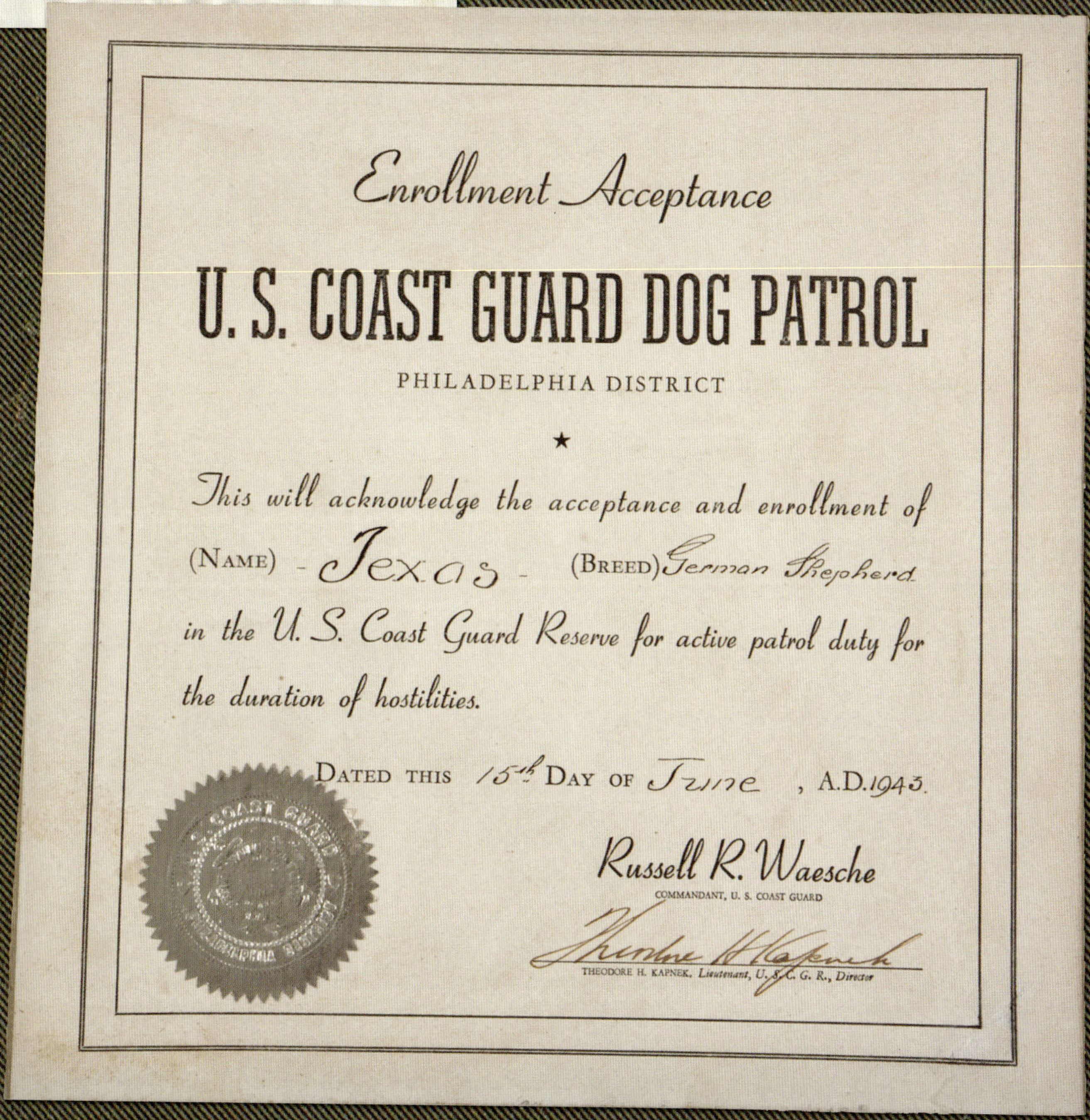

Enrollment Acceptance

U. S. COAST GUARD DOG PATROL

PHILADELPHIA DISTRICT

★

This will acknowledge the acceptance and enrollment of

(NAME) - Texas - (BREED) German Shepherd

in the U.S. Coast Guard Reserve for active patrol duty for the duration of hostilities.

DATED THIS 15th DAY OF June, A.D. 1943.

Russell R. Waesche
COMMANDANT, U. S. COAST GUARD

Theodore H. Kapnek
THEODORE H. KAPNEK, *Lieutenant, U. S. C. G. R., Director*

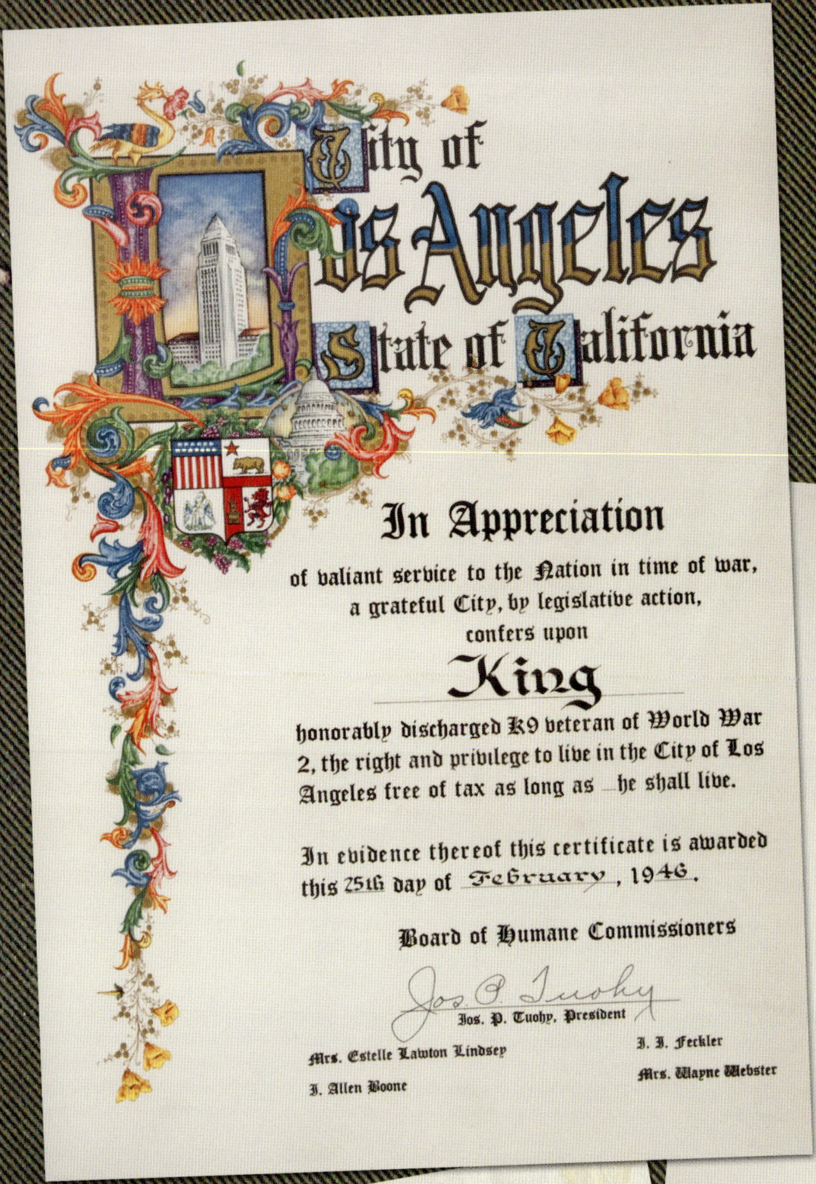

City of
Los Angeles
State of California

In Appreciation

of valiant service to the Nation in time of war, a grateful City, by legislative action, confers upon

King

honorably discharged K9 veteran of World War 2, the right and privilege to live in the City of Los Angeles free of tax as long as he shall live.

In evidence thereof this certificate is awarded this 25th day of February, 1946.

Board of Humane Commissioners

Jos. P. Tuohy, President

Mrs. Estelle Lawton Lindsey — J. J. Feckler

J. Allen Boone — Mrs. Wayne Webster

CITY OF LOS ANGELES APPRECIATION CERTIFICATE

was given to "King", a U.S. Army K-9, with a period photo of him laying on the top of his U.S. Army shipping crate (see picture right). *Authors collection.*

FIRST DAY OF ISSUE ENVELOPES AND POST CARDS

CHAPTER 6

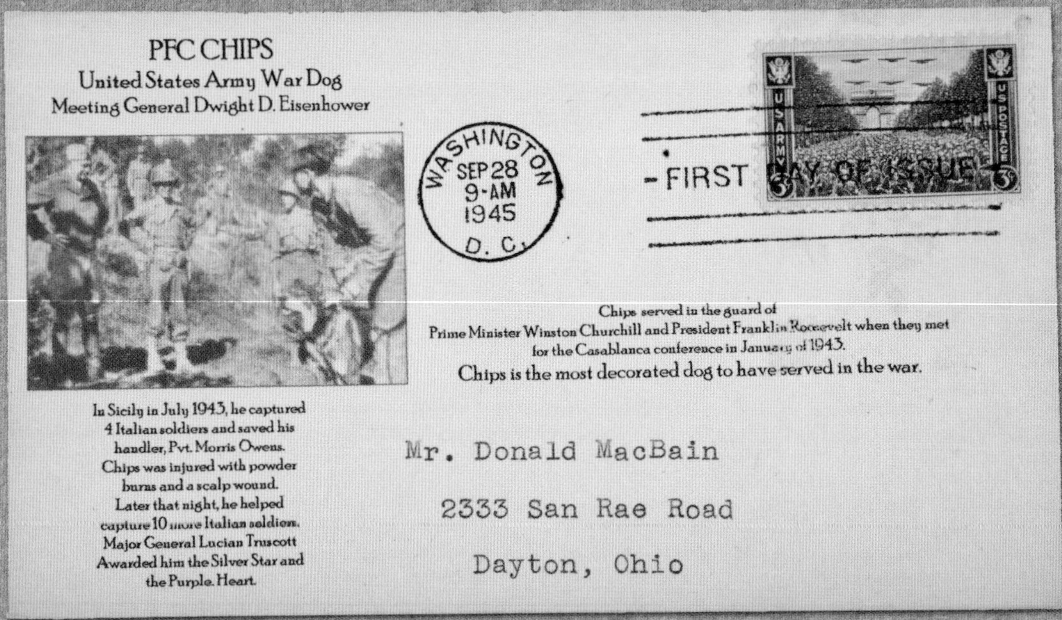

WAR DOG FIRST DAY OF ISSUE POSTAL COVERS

Authors collection

WAR DOG FIRST DAY OF ISSUE POSTAL COVERS

Authors collection

WAR DOG FIRST DAY OF ISSUE POSTAL COVERS

Authors collection

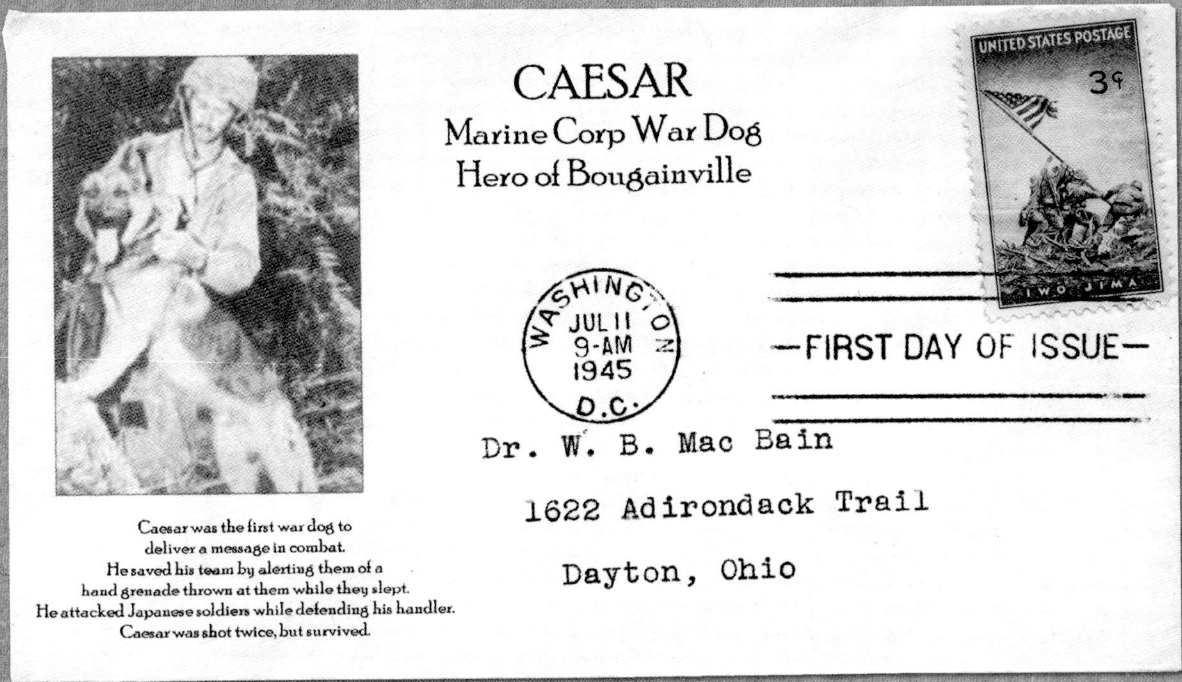

WAR DOG FIRST DAY OF ISSUE POSTAL COVERS

Authors collection

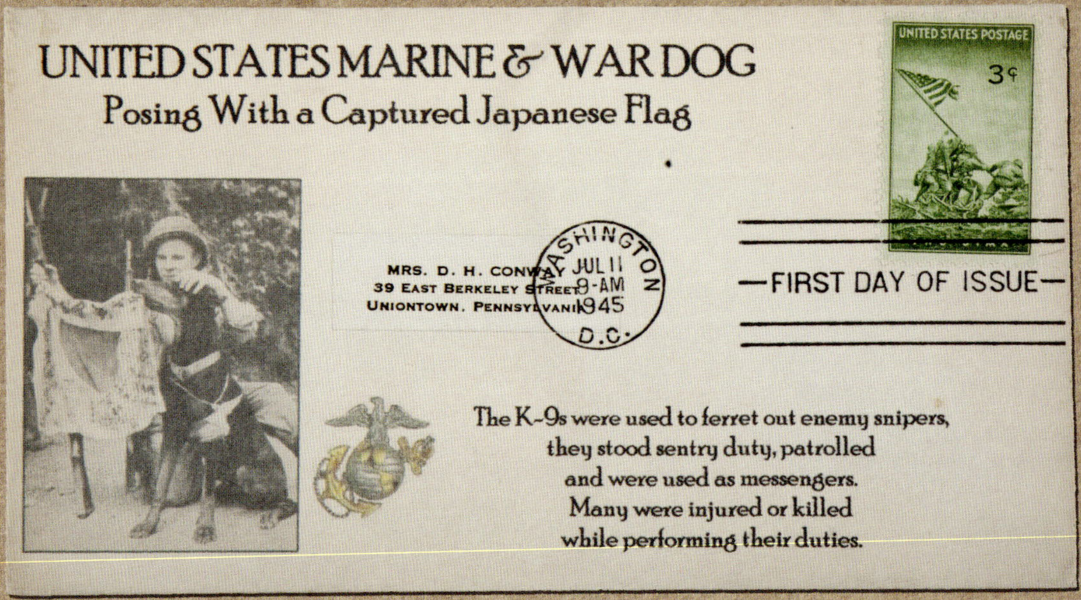

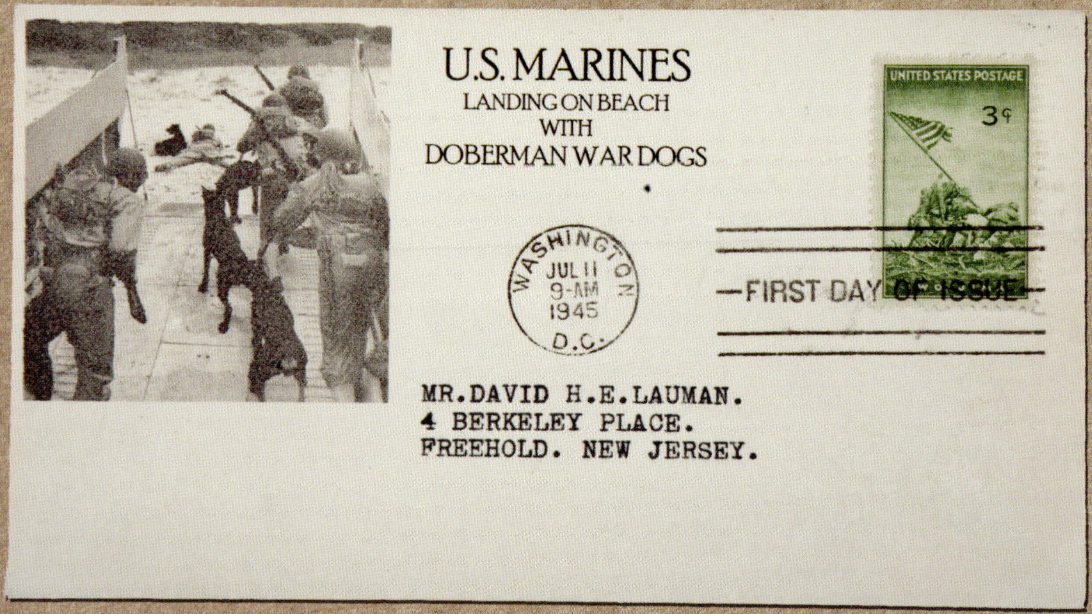

WAR DOG FIRST DAY OF ISSUE POSTAL COVERS

Authors collection

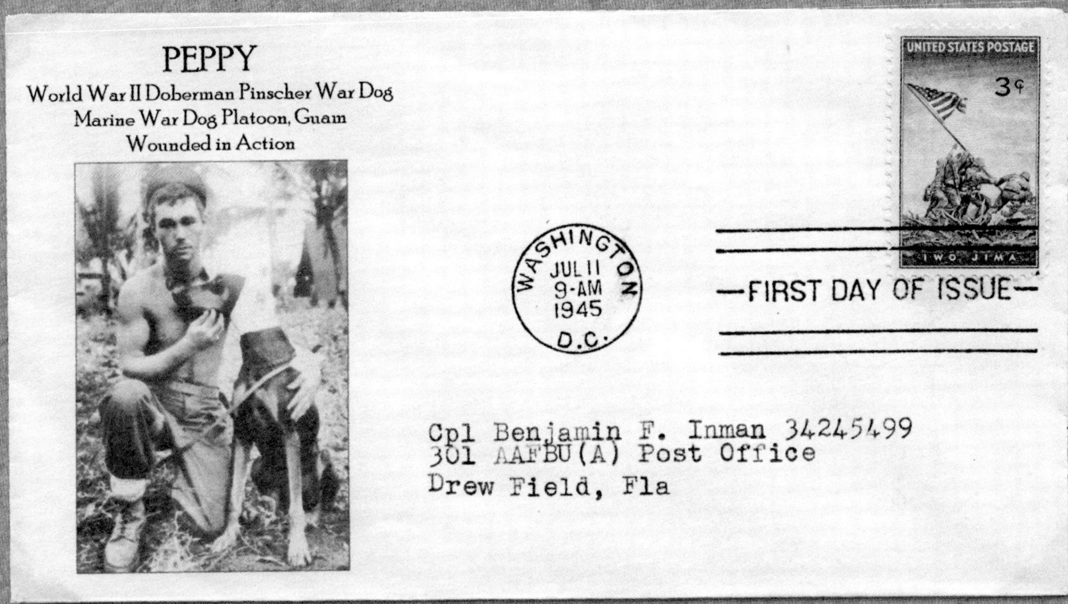

WAR DOG FIRST DAY OF ISSUE POSTAL COVERS

Authors collection

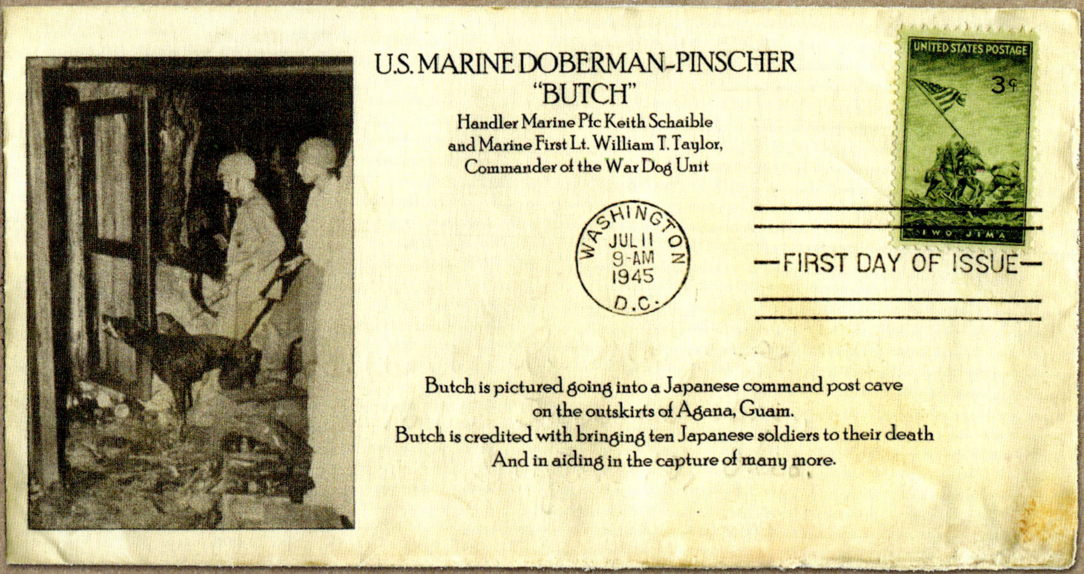

WAR DOG FIRST DAY OF ISSUE POSTAL COVERS

Authors collection

WAR DOG FIRST DAY OF ISSUE POSTAL COVERS

Authors collection

K-9 CORPS WAR DOG PATRIOTIC ENVELOPE ARTWORK

Authors collection

POST CARD

WWII postcard of the K-9 detachment at Fort Snelling, Minnesota. *Authors collection*

POST CARD

of a trainer and his K-9 at Fort McPherson, Atlanta, Georgia. *Authors collection*

POST CARD

of the U.S. Army remount depot at Front Royal, Virginia, which was used as a war dog training and reception center during WWII. *Authors collection*

POST CARD

of war dogs on duty at Camp Atterbury, Indiana. *Authors collection*

POSTCARD OF THE WAR DOG CEMETERY ON GUAM

containing the 25 war dogs that were killed during the invasion of Guam. *Authors collection*

DOGS FOR DEFENSE RECRUITING ENVELOPE ARTWORK

Authors collection

DOGS FOR DEFENSE WAR DOG FUND POST CARD

Authors collection

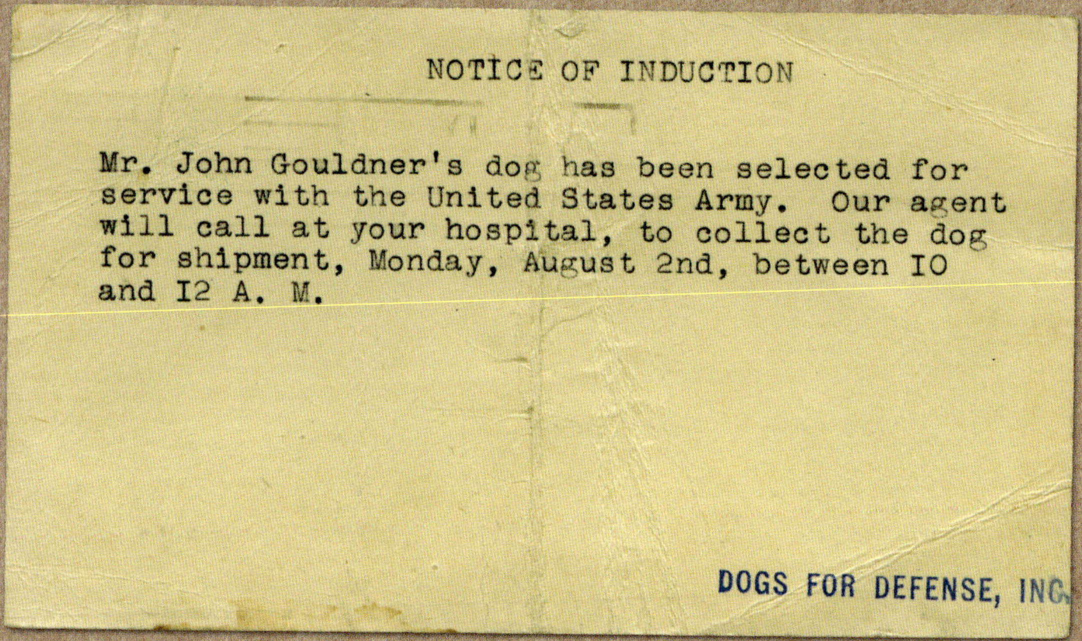

NOTICE OF INDUCTION

Mr. John Gouldner's dog has been selected for service with the United States Army. Our agent will call at your hospital, to collect the dog for shipment, Monday, August 2nd, between 10 and 12 A. M.

DOGS FOR DEFENSE, INC.

NOTICE OF INDUCTION POSTCARD

was used by Dogs for Defense to notify the donor that their dog was selected for service in the U.S. Army. *Courtesy Hayes Otoupalik*

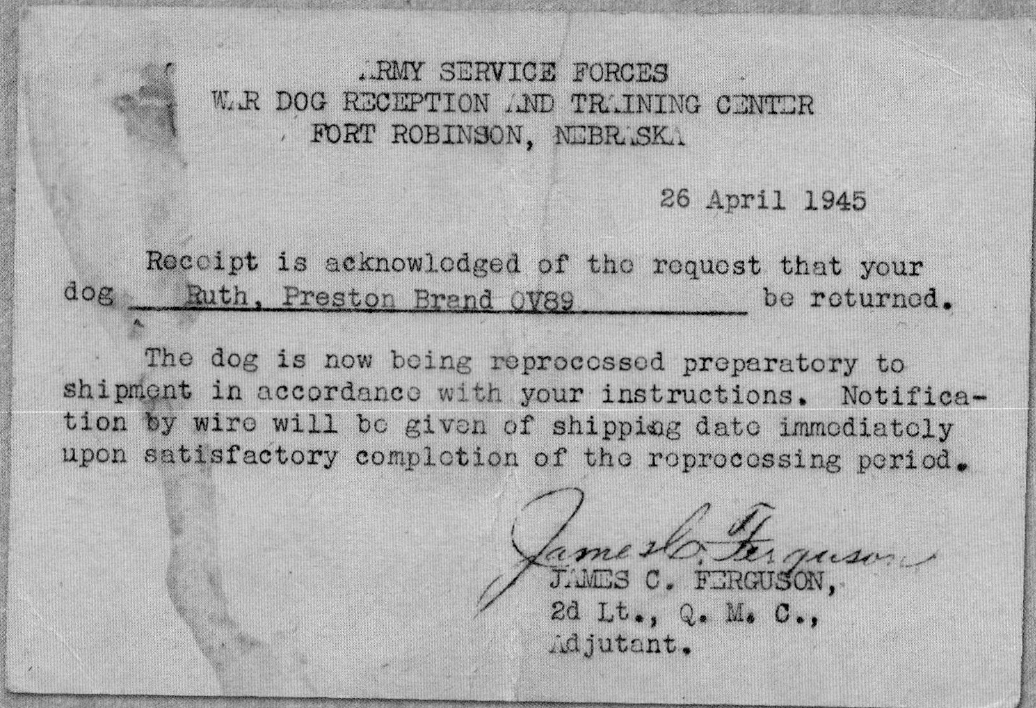

ARMY SERVICE FORCES
WAR DOG RECEPTION AND TRAINING CENTER
FORT ROBINSON, NEBRASKA

26 April 1945

Receipt is acknowledged of the request that your dog Ruth, Preston Brand 0V89 be returned.

The dog is now being reprocessed preparatory to shipment in accordance with your instructions. Notification by wire will be given of shipping date immediately upon satisfactory completion of the reprocessing period.

James C. Ferguson
JAMES C. FERGUSON,
2d Lt., Q. M. C.,
Adjutant.

RECEIPT OF REQUEST TO RETURN A WAR DOG

As the war was ending, the Department of Defense sent this receipt to the donor if the donor had originally wanted the dog back after its service was completed. If the dog was healthy it would be sent to a facility to be detrained for civilian life. Then the dog would be returned to its original donor if the training was successful.
Courtesy Hayes Otoupalik

FLEET MARINE FORCE, PACIFIC, DOG PLATOON SHOULDER PATCH

Each platoon consisted of 18 messenger and 18 scout dogs with one officer and 65 enlisted men. *Authors collection*

DOG AND HORSE HANDLER USCG RATING BADGES

used during WWII. These ratings came in third class, second class, first class, and chief petty officer. These ratings were manufactured for the white uniform, the blue uniform, and in bullion. *Authors collection*

BIBLIOGRAPHY

FM 25-6: Dog Transportation. 19 August 1944.

TM 10-396: War Dogs. 1 July 1943.

Behan, John M. *Dogs of War*. 1946.

Dempewolff, Richard. *Animal Reveille*. 1943.

Downey, Fairfax. *Dogs for Defense, American dogs in the Second World War, 1942-1945*. 1955.

Going, Clayton G. *Dogs at War*. 1945.

Young, Thomas. *Dogs for Democracy*. 1944.

INFORMATION WANTED

Any help in identifying this unknown insignia would be greatly appreciated. The insignia is made of brass with two screw back posts on the back and measures 1 ½" in diameter.

Anyone with additional information about items contained in this book or any other information on WWII U.S. war dogs, please contact the author at WARDOGMILITARIA.COM.